TESTIMONIALS

With each student and every story, Marena skillfully teaches us the keys to navigate difficulties, suffering, and despair are the same: grit, grace, and faith.

— SD Ferguson,
Author *Journey Back to Me; Touring the Landscape of my Mind.*

The author was grounded by her rural Midwestern roots. As a nursing instructor she met head on the volatility that fractured the youth of her community. She offers us a vivid perspective of human love infused into fragile youth. Sharing her experiences, she engages us with the pain of her students compelling us to continue reading and perhaps to share the story. This is a great book club offering.

— Elizabeth Belenchia,
Author *My Walk to The Water*

The author vividly shares moving experiences with her students. She does this with insight, respect, and compassion, while offering wise philosophy from the heart.

This sensitively written account is perfect for sharing with family and friends.

The descriptive details bring Marena's narrative to life. It's like watching a movie.

— Pam Horrisberger,
Book Club Member and inveterate reader.

Superbly written! The author transports us into the lives of others, not unlike our own. Her uncanny ability to find the humor and compassion in very real and timely topics allows the us to find the humanness in the characters as well as ourselves.

—Dana Tongdangjoue, Founder, EquiYoga

UNLOCKING
September

Marena J. White

26 25 24 23 22 21   1 2 3 4 5 6 7 8

UNLOCKING SEPTEMBER
Copyright © 2021 MARENA J. WHITE

Names and identifying characteristics of people mentioned in this book have been changed to protect the privacy of those individuals.

Published by:
Emerge Publishing, LLC
9521 B Riverside parkway, Suite 243
Tulsa, OK 74137
Phone: 888.407.4447 www.emerge.pub

Library of Congress Cataloging-in-Publication Data:
ISBN: 978-1-949758-59-7 Perfect Bound

Printed in the United States

Dedicated
to
my husband William,
who shared my life and faith,
who understood my heart.

CONTENTS

Part Three
a time to weep, and a time to laugh; a time to mourn, and a time to dance...
Ecclesiastes 3:4 ESV

Part Four
a time to cast away stones, and a time to gather stones together; a time to embrace, and a time to refrain from embracing... Ecclesiastes 3:5 ESV

Part Five
a time to seek, and a time to lose; a time to keep, and a time to cast away...
Ecclesiastes 3:6 ESV

Part Six

a time to tear, and a time to sew; a time to keep silence, and a time to speak... Ecclesiastes 3:7 ESV

Part Seven

a time to love, and a time to hate; a time for war, and a time for peace. Ecclesiastes 3:8 ESV

Part Eight

So I saw that there is nothing better than that a man should rejoice in his work, for that is his lot. Who can bring him to see what will be after him? Ecclesiastes 3:22 ESV

ACKNOWLEDGEMENTS

Jacob, my student, I will never forget the day you approached my desk and encouraged me to write about your classmates. You lamented their struggles, the need for their stories to be told, and you spoke the words to my heart that inspired me to write this book.

The challenge in writing these stories was to make each one as true as possible without offering information that might violate individual privacy. I changed every name of every character, including my own. I changed non-critical events and descriptions in respect of privacy. I changed the names of places. Six stories are composites. The meaning of each story remains.

William, my beloved husband, thank you for standing by me through the crazy days of my writing and for committing yourself to the time we shared. Your support and insights led to the project's completion. My life was so much happier and more meaningful with your love, support, and wisdom. Being my husband was not an easy job. I always loved only you and always will, and I miss you deeply.

My love to our daughters, who remain the lights of my life and will always be my greatest joys. Thank you for your encouragement and the time spent reading, correcting, rereading, and commenting on my writing, but, most of all, thank you for listening. Thanks to my sons-in-law for providing the humor I needed on rough days.

To Lara, my mentor, and her parents, Jack and Lucy: Thanks for your never-ending reinforcement and enthusiasm for taking my vague notions and turning them into projects of substance. Your guidance and diligence made this book a reality, and Sheila, your unwavering support and willingness to read my stories and give me honest feedback are most appreciated. I will not forget our writing club time. Elizabeth you gave intuitive sparks that led me to think more deeply as I wrote.

A special THANK YOU to Stone for an excellent Cover Design and to Jordyn for suggesting a variety of names to be used in my writing.

I thank the ladies of my book club dearly for being so responsive to my efforts: listening to my stories, offering thoughts, and allowing me to babble on about my work. A noted thank you to Pam and Julie for reading my stories and providing feedback.

A special thank you to my longtime friend, Gloria, who challenged me to write one story at a time. She read each one and always responded, "Keep writing." I am grateful for you pushing me along.

And when I thought I couldn't finish, it was my band of three friends, the Rosekateers, Jackie, Mary Ellen and Colette, who cheered me on and refused to let me quit. And thank you, Colette and Kathy, for introducing me to my editor, Amanda Hamilton.

Amanda, a skilled professional, took my verbose, wandering stories and helped me turn them into powerful reflections. Without her guidance and expertise, this book would never have taken form. Thank you for being such a pleasure to work with.

Acknowledgement and love to my remarkable publishing team at Emerge: Brian Marketing Director, Julie, Production Manager, Randy, Sales Manager and Brook, Social Media and Ad Marketer.

Ultimately the greatest thanks belong to my students, from whom I learned about the suffering of the human heart. I believe that the quality of thoughts determines the quality of life, but in my blessed world of God, peace, hope, joy, family, and love, I could not fathom how students consumed by fear, hunger, pain, violence, failure, or abuse experienced life. Each day's disruptions, no matter how sorrowful, tense, threatening, or confusing, became opportunities to clear away the dregs of weakness, fear, complacency, and hopeless resignation that all of life is unfair. I thought working through today's suffering would prevent them from drowning in tomorrow's devastations. But the healing process was a long road, one whose end we didn't always reach.

I just needed one small key to open the heart and set it free.

INTRODUCTION

I can't do this anymore. The words echoed my thoughts the day I faced reality and resigned from my nursing position. My work was no longer in step with my heart.

"Make a difference in the world," my father had said. But what had I done to do that?

It wasn't until I sat on the bleachers watching my daughters compete in a tri-county track meet that I uncovered my true calling.

I saw him at various school sports events as he dragged his six-year-old daughter by her arm about the track with his wife following behind, head bowed low. Their clothes were crumpled and his shoes had holes in the toes. The child and wife exposed bruises of various size, shape, and color.

He, his wife, and daughter sat two rows down from us. His daughter became restless, fidgeting in her seat and pulling his pant leg and tugging her mother's housedress. He waved his hand in her face and spoke loudly at the mother, although I could not hear his words. His neck veins pulsed as he looked daggers at his precious little girl. The child whimpered. He slapped her across the face so hard she fell between the bleacher seats to the ground below. His wife hesitated then stood to make her way to the child. He pushed her back down onto the bleacher seat.

Those present watched in shock. Someone needs to speak up, protect the child, I thought. No one moved. I found myself heading for the screaming little girl. Behind me I heard two sets of footsteps of which one was my husband Liam's. I assumed the other was this heartless man's steps pounding the pavement. I sat beside this precious child in the gravel, picked up her frail body, and held her on my lap, rocking. Her dirty clothes smelled like cigarettes, wet dog, and urine. As she began to speak through the sobs, I noticed a speech delay. Liam and I stayed with her. And when the man tried to take her, I held her tightly.

"You have no right to slap this child and shouldn't be near her," I cried out.

Liam intervened. I was relieved to be able to temporarily protect her and grateful that Liam was there to protect me.

A moment later the crowd roared and I knew we'd missed something good. But then I wondered, What will this child miss? Who will speak for and protect her, nourish and educate her, give her love and hope?

When the meet was over the little girl's mother, in the same condition as her daughter, came and carried her away.

It was then that I was called to teach.

＝⧑⧒＝

Five months after I resigned from the hospital and three months after my first vocational education college program course, I began teaching.

As my car coasted along the winding street, I noticed the vibrant green leaves of summer fading to shades of purple, red, orange, and brown. I slowed the car to savor the scenery.

The aging one-story yellow cinder block school sprawled across the top of a hill like a lost, forgotten child. Tall single-pane windows flanked with dirty white casing peppered the edifice, a rhino could shuffle through the main double doors, and gloomy pea-green lockers lined the mismatched painted halls that extended like arms and legs from a central command point. Yet the design radiated a subliminal cheerfulness.

The health careers classroom and lab, my room, was at the far end of the longest passageway. The custodian, Kalen, walked with me. Creases earned over time, wrinkles projected from the outer corner of each eye, and furrows circling his mouth and chin adorned his face. He seemed like a busy man, a man wise with years, and far more than the Keeper of the Keys, as he referred to himself.

Ch'trik. Kalen unlocked my door but I hesitated. Emptiness rushed at me and doubts overcame me, yet I smiled an obligatory smile. Lost in my own world, I startled when Kalen's keys jingled as he removed a small ring of five keys, my keys: for the building, the office, the work room, my classroom, and my office.

"Bring these with you every day," Kalen instructed. "And do not lose them. You have to return them to me at the end of the year." After a pause, he continued, "Everybody has keys. It's what you do with them that counts."

Keys unlock doors, I thought. But I asked politely, "What do you mean?"

"It's what you do each September, which doors you open."

There are five doors for me to open, I thought, stuck on literalism.

"You see, you can use them to keep pieces of the world out. Or you can use them to let pieces of the world in. You can open the hearts and minds of students and sometimes even parents," he said.

"Oh," I said, following his wisdom.

"Use them wisely. Define yourself with your keys, by who and what is out or in. Those on the inside become distinct voices and memories. And sure, there's tears and laughter, pain and joy, failure and success. That's reality."

"What about those who don't enter and the world they won't open?" I asked.

"They're challenges, but always have a door unlocked for them," he said, turning and walking away.

My classroom was sectioned into two large rooms, divided by a row of cinder blocks and windows. Off-white walls painted a cloudy, colorless environment. Floor-to-ceiling white cabinets and countertops covered two walls in the first room. I pulled back torn, faded curtains to reveal lockers that blended with the walls. In a far corner rested a dilapidated dental chair surrounded by twenty-six vintage student desks, each with a hard plastic chair. And a grainy green chalkboard stretched across the front of the lab. In the closet-sized room to the right of the chalkboard was a vintage teacher's desk and metal chair and a four-drawer filing cabinet, dented from years of wear and tear.

The second room consisted of base cabinets only, two walls with windows, a door to the outside, and a 1960s hospital bed. Sunlight, filtered through the attached greenhouse, radiated through the windows. Signs of a retired horticulture lab, I noted.

What have I done? Students arrive in four days and I've inherited a hand-me-down lab with no working equipment, textbooks, or supplies. Why did I leave nursing?

⚔

Four exhausting days later, I sauntered into the building, my old messenger bag—stuffed with papers, books, and my first day's class preparation—over my shoulder. My legs moved as if I dragged fifty pounds on each. I counted the steps to the main entrance: 372. After another 369 the ominous scratched and dented lab door was before me. I entered the vast empty space where teenage students would soon learn skilled trades in health technologies.

What am I doing here? I thought, shaking my head.

Forty-five minutes later clusters of students meandered toward my classroom. I perspired a hidden sweat and considered locking the door and sprinting away.

Twenty-five hormone-fortified females, each distinctive in a collective sort of way, gave me narrow-eyed half smiles. One wore a baby doll dress over leggings, another was in a black bodysuit covered with a striped sweater, and the others were clothed in ripped blue jean overalls with the straps down. Hair hung straight or was cut short in flipped-out bobs. Four girls feathered their hair and others let it drape around their faces. All was done in the name of fashion to impress one another without regard for their true selves because those not adhering to this teen code received stares and endured alone.

Some students walked a graceful path and others bore perpetual stoops. I heard gum chomping and candy crunching amid the tall, short, slender, and sturdy builds with brightly painted nails decorated with ornaments. The girls wore makeup and bruises, and I displayed a white power suit—my uniform and lab coat.

I had reviewed growth and development through the teen years and mulled over educational and nursing theories until I saw stars, but still, a hidden turbulence pulsed through my veins. I hid the tremor in my voice and willed my body to move and smile even as my voice cracked.

━╪╫━

I survived the first nerve-racking day and life at school fell into an unpredictable routine as I observed each student's individuality, needs, and character. I was all too aware that students who attend a vocational school or career center often are not considered to be hard-working serious students. They sometimes become educational system throwaways. But I refused to let that happen.

The students that chose my lab carried baggage of various shapes and sizes—scars from childhood bug bites—and they reshuffled the weight of it as they entered school each day. Those creepy-crawlies that snuck in on the fur of a pet, hid in grass, and sat on leaves nibbled a piece at a time, gravitated to the weak and vulnerable, and became an epidemic of the soul. Weighted damage placed fear behind students' eyes and buried secrets in their souls.

The uncertainties of academic difficulties, appearance, and underage sex; suspicions from mental and emotional issues; and the horrors of addiction and bullying were shadows in my classroom. Deeply tucked in unseen compartments, disease—from broken homes, mental illness, stress, abuse, loss, rape, neglect, depression, and poverty—flourished. But the symptoms were visible. Nothing could have prepared me for the world I had entered.

Our days in the classroom competed with the ticking clock. Early on I struggled to balance my demanding expectations with a sense of community and connection. It took two years to develop my teacher voice—to speak with authority, lecture accurately, and practice with the heart. That voice became a part of me and has given me vision ever since.

I taught students a subject rather than teaching the subject to students. I educated rather than preaching at students to learn. I used the nursing process instead of the educational theories I'd been force-fed, and I developed lessons that related to each student's career goals to challenge and engage them. And, when necessary, I repeated lessons using a different method.

I cultivated connections between the students' lives and mine, and I respected them as individuals. We learned to laugh and cry together, discuss our differences, celebrate successes, and forgive each other.

My students had piercing honesty. I listened to their words and their hearts. Forging my path with them was not easy nor was it always successful. Students resisted, classes fragmented, colleagues disagreed with my techniques, and I failed often.

But each day students entered and exited through a door where they could become someone—a door locked and unlocked with the keys I embraced: Kalen's keys. It was just what I did with them each September.

PART ONE

For everything there is a season,
and a time for every matter under the heaven
a time to be born, and a time to die;
a time to plant, and a time to pluck up that which is planted;

Ecclesiastes 3:1-2 ESV

A BARREN WORLD

A nurse in green scrubs escorted me to Kelsie's room, then placed baby Zachary in her arms to feed. Kelsie had entered motherhood deserted by those close to her heart. Bottles, pacifiers, grating squeals, sleepless nights, and diaper rash were her new reality.

Nine months earlier Kelsie had stridden into my classroom garbed in a navy blouse, jeans, and a pair of oxford platforms. Her hazel eyes projected a gentle aura. Her work was exceptional and she embodied many positive character traits.

It was mid-year when she fell prey to a young man who called himself Z. Her grades dropped, angry outbursts began, and relationships with classmates went awry. Z seduced her with fantasies and lies, drawing her away from her parents and other encouragers in her life. Scrapes with the law—car crashes and illegal drug and alcohol abuse—became the new norm.

I cautioned her but Kelsie grew silent, resisting every word. She loved Z. From her perspective he was powerful, made her feel good, and had plenty of money.

"I am Z's girl," she said. "He loves me. Says I'm not good enough for any other guy. I'm all his and he'll be with me forever."

But she lost herself in his deception when her mistakes became excuses for him hitting her. And the downward spiral continued.

One day after lab Kelsie closed my office door and hung the Do Not Disturb sign she had given me over the knob. I saw the collection of blood under her left eye through layers of makeup as shadows of blue and violet crossed to her left ear. Last week it had been the right eye.

Kelsie gave me her only excuse. "I walked into a door. I'm clumsy."

"I don't believe that, Kelsie. Tell the truth so we can get you help. Z's nineteen, an adult. You know he's a drug supplier? And why nickname himself with a letter, a low status letter? What's he hiding from?"

She tried to swallow a lump of tears but poured out her heart instead.

"I'm not alone. I mean, there's people everywhere, but…well, I feel lonely. Z won't let me talk to anybody, not even my parents. I have to tell him where I am all the time. Yeah, I know about the drugs. He's had me using them and drinking lots. My parents locked me in my room, but I went out through the window."

"Did your parents' and grandmother's love run away too?" I asked.

Tears began streaming down her face.

"I haven't talked to Grandma in so long and I love her," she cried. "She always had time to be with me. I wish I could change what's happened. I'm sad all the time, I hurt the ones I love and who love me, and now I'm pregnant. I don't want a baby and thought I'd give it away, but Z wants me to get an abortion. I don't know what to do. That's why he hit me."

"Perhaps you would like to talk with our Graduation, Reality, and Dual-Role Skills (GRADS) counselor," I suggested. "She can help you look into adoption. And Z doesn't have to attend."

"I don't need any counseling. He'll always be with me. He won't leave me or this baby."

"Do you think you should tell your parents?"

Through tears she said, "They won't care."

"I'm concerned for you and the baby," I pleaded. "Z's violence and drug use will not end and may even escalate. Do you want the baby exposed to dealing or drug use in the home? Are you willing to be beaten in front of your child or perhaps have the child abused? You need a safe place."

But Kelsie envisioned romance and love, not the impending pain.

Kelsie's mother phoned me after learning her daughter was expecting.

"I want you to know Kelsie caused her own problems taking drugs, drinking, and running around with those friends of hers," her mother said. "I tried to talk to her but she wouldn't listen and went to her room, so we locked her in. A few nights ago she wanted me to hug her. Well, it was too late for that."

I told her we had help at school for Kelsie, but she didn't listen.

"Kelsie's innocence is dead," she continued. "This girl who sleeps with the light on at night, can't cook, and knows nothing about keeping a home is going to be a mother. Well, she'll have to learn without me. The time for babying her is over."

"This love can't be easy," I said. "Motherhood never is. But this is a defining moment for you and your husband: you'll be grandparents. Plus, Kelsie needs you and she wants you if you can just find forgiveness in your heart and help her. She really needs your love and support."

"I'm not ashamed of making her responsible. She needs to grow up. I'm not ashamed of not comforting her. I am ashamed that Kelsie's pregnant. Life isn't easy, but this is her problem. She ruined her life and mine."

Kelsie's mom's heart was hard.

Z threw Kelsie away like a piece of trash, beaten and broken. By April all family and friends had deserted her, leaving her in a barren world, devoid of love.

"Out of life's dark places opportunities can arise," I reminded her, pointing to the twenty-third Psalm poster on my office bulletin board. But this life was not what she wanted.

When Zachary was twenty days old, Kelsie quit school and became a statistic. She and Zachary lived with her grandmother, who supported them but was unable to physically care for the baby.

Kelsie phoned me often. Life was a constant drone.

"Zachary cries and whines," she said. "I'm exhausted and get little sleep. He takes all my time 'cause I play with him and read some little books. Grandma says it's normal and that he'll grow."

Kelsie reported on life, a life she was learning was not all about her. She no longer remembered who she used to be, now living in sparse surroundings and feeling abandoned.

Her only joy came in bits of hope.

The following February, Zachary, Kelsie, Grandma, and I met at a local coffee shop. Kelsie wore sweats. I noticed cracks and cuts over her fingers and her nails were well-bitten and barely visible. Zachary's toys invaded the table as we discussed motherhood. It was easy to focus on the hard parts but the blessings of giggles, hugs, and kisses made the sacrifices well worth it.

I spoke to Kelsie about her future. "Have you considered getting your GED?"

"There is no time."

"You could do some of the work online. Perhaps there is some-one who could watch Zachary when you need to attend a class. You at least need a high school diploma to get a job."

Kelsie said, "All this fuss about my diploma?"

I explained a bit more of the new online program supported by her school district but Kelsie's self-doubt was evident.

"Do this for Zachary," I pleaded. "Improve your lives."

In the end Kelsie agreed and finished in late summer, Grandma beaming with pride.

I drafted a letter of recommendation for Kelsie and she was accepted into the two-year radiology tech program at the local community college, but her self-doubt and loneliness continued to isolate her as she studied at home.

Three years later, though, she graduated. And four years after graduation, she phoned me again.

"I work in the hospital now," Kelsie said. "I enjoy the work and the pay and benefits are good. Zachary starts first grade next month. Dad and I talk a little. He thinks Mom will come around. I want you to know I go to church now. It's a Methodist church I walk to. I've learned so much from life, from Grandma, and from you. I just didn't listen. And motherhood is a special gift, a love with no equal. At my church and at work I try to help other young mothers—those who are in the wasteland of desolation. It's not hopeless."

FLOWERS WILT

In front of me lay the entryway to Traditions Funeral Home. I entered through the giant golden door, scanned the crowded room, and found the registry.

I weaved a slow path toward Brady's family—his mother, father, and older sister, Jaimie. Melancholy hung in the room as an arctic cold moved in. I spoke garbled words through hugs and tears. Where is the comfort in this grief and anguish?

The next day we all crowded again into the conventional space: my forty-nine students and Brady's classmates, friends, and school faculty and staff.

The air was limp and candlelight flickered as though darkness surrounded us. Brady and his family would never embrace again. Small solemn cards on flower arrangements offered sympathy and rose casket sprays and gentle baskets of mums and lilies gave the impression of life, but even their petals had begun to droop, setting in motion a final descent.

I stood in front of the casket with a sense of emptiness. Brady looked asleep and innocent. Why, of all people, a teenager? A blue streak of hair hugged his rugged face, and his words echoed through my thoughts.

"I love this class...It's really helping me...I can talk with classmates now...Never thought I'd come to a vocational school...I even have friends here...I don't like my home high school...I get made fun of...bullied...I like my nails painted, my hair dyed...I just ignore it all...I have to ride the bus to that school and now they wait for me...They just won't leave me alone."

⚬

Earlier in the school year, Brady had discussed his worries with me.

"Last year a bunch of boys flung spitballs at me and barked gay slurs," he said. "They called me disgusting and told me I was a thing. And I never knew what might happen at lunchtime. It was miserable. Once somebody filmed me at the zoo and put it on Facebook like I was the star attraction. It was easier to go outside to eat or hide in the bathroom than to be humiliated."

"Brady, you need to tell your parents," I urged.

He did that same evening, and I reported his situation to administration as well. Brady said the harassment would get worse, though, and it did. While it stopped during school hours, it escalated afterward.

Five days ago no one knew how Brady had happened upon his father's gun. No one heard the cold snap of the trigger. No one watched his bright room wane to a liquid and musical rhythm, free of harshness and friction, now forever gray.

⚬

The service began as "Amazing Grace," "Nearer My God to Thee," and "Rock of Ages" circled and imparted a peace about the room.

Brady's pastor and youth leader spoke.

"We are here today to pay tribute and respect to…We are here today to show love and support for…Finally we are here today to seek and receive comfort…And the peace of God, which passes all understanding…"

They and Brady shared faith.

Then Jaimie shared stories from her childhood with Brady: secrets they shared, battles they fought, and memories of birthdays, holiday celebrations, parties, laughter, and love.

She and Brady shared their hearts.

Brady's best friend, George, was the last to speak. He reminisced about games they played, races they ran, parties they attended, and their childhood friendship.

George and Brady shared time.

The hearse arrived and the funeral parlor employees closed and sealed the casket, snuffed out the wavering candle flames, and removed the wilting flowers. Petals fell unheeded as the procession commenced. Some joined while others lingered in the chill. I exited the backdrop of tears and sobs, noticing even the grass beginning to wither.

Monday arrived and the gloom lingered as students loitered about my desk talking. I had never seen students bully him, but Marc, a classmate, had.

"We didn't defend him when we had the chance," he said. "You know, at our home school and even here in the cafeteria."

All students agreed as Brady's death choked the room. Queasiness overcame me. For me to teach, students to learn, and class to be productive, I had to do something.

Trained counselors were available in the school cafeteria, but my students declined sharing with someone they did not know. So I listened calmly to their sorrow and grief. Brady's classmates would move on from this sad moment. But they would not forget.

A week later I phoned Brady's family.

"We live every day reminded of and sorrowful for Brady's death," his mother told me. "We recall good times, funny moments, and his kindness. Jaimie now spends time with our pastor in counseling and praying. She's getting more involved in church activities."

It was a good conversation, as good as one of that nature could be. Yet one remark haunted me.

"He thought he was friendless, you know, lonesome," his mom said. "Where were all the students and others when he hurt so badly?"

I lay awake that night wondering, Did we really know Brady? Or was he just another student? Did we listen, allow him to be heard? What did we miss? I did not want to feel sad, but my thoughts ran amuck and my heart was heavy.

Through the week several colleagues reminded me that I couldn't save everyone. But Brady was not everyone. He grew up playing baseball and had fond memories until high school when he was outed by a friend he had trusted with his secret. Brady was made fun of and his team yelled profanities and threatened to beat him up. Traumatized, he quit the team, hating himself and life.

One degraded and lonely child cried for help. Did anyone hear?

BURNT WEEDS

The shop was a small Bohemian boutique wedged between a musty antique store and a local art gallery. I stumbled upon it accidently and curiosity led me inside.

Glancing about the store I noticed beads in the back room doorway and the clutter of notions, odds and ends, and hippy-style clothing and accessories. A flash of memories flooded my mind, a flash of different times.

I detected singed rope and burnt weeds, a lingering smoky smell. The beads clattered as the salesclerk stepped out. Around her neck dangled a peace necklace, and matching earrings swung from her ears. She wore a macramé-trimmed vibrant floral paisley baby doll dress, accented by high earthy boots adorned with beads and laces.

"Hi, may I help you?" the flowerchild said.

Immediately I recognized Blossom, my former student.

⊷⊱⊰⊶

Just five years ago Blossom sat in my office after lab had ended for the day.

"No reason I'm here, jus' wanna talk," she said.

We discussed the latest movies to start, but that quickly progressed to quirky conversation.

Blossom said, "My mother is a lesbian."

I fumbled for what to say and asked her to explain.

Willingly, Blossom unfolded more than I bargained for.

"Mom spent several years in prison an' she has a girlfriend. They're both Wiccan so I became Wiccan like them."

My mouth dropped open, my eyes widened, and my hand went to my throat. She must have noticed my shock.

"I'm a white witch, a believer of the enchantment."

At that point I simply said, "Oh."

"I learned the laws and use them. Wiccans have weekly meetings. It's the coven I joined where I've learned their magical ways. After a year of study, I moved through the dedication ritual and now I even write a journal of my experiences. You like us to journal about our lives so that's what I've been doing. I just can't stop talking about it. We form a Wiccan circle and chant, pray, and contact spirits from beyond. I built my own altar to worship at with candles and our icons. I've learned to cast spells but only good ones, kind ones. I'm gonna change the world."

Unable to decipher my emotions, I remained speechless.

She talked of being free with sex, having no boundaries. She told me that sex is a "healthy, physical expression of love among us."

I called that manipulation.

We sat together in silence and as Blossom prepared to leave, I asked if I could pray for her soul. She scowled, turned, and stomped out of the room.

A few days later Blossom entered the lab early in the morning and placed a hemp-chained necklace with a silver five-pointed star within a circle on my desk.

"It's a Wiccan symbol that represents the five elements: earth, air, water, fire, and spirit," Blossom explained.

I knew it as satanic and grimaced.

Blossom never discussed our previous conversation. Yet over time we shared our different beliefs. I told her of my Christian faith—who I was, what I had become because of my faith, and what I cherished most of all. She talked of her coven and told me of her activities. She followed spirits and kept searching, and that gave me hope.

It was the middle of the night after Blossom and I had our last conversation that I tossed and turned. A trickle of moonlight filtered through the window while my thoughts kept me awake.

Her problems would get bigger, not better. New faces would interweave with the same struggles of others. Blossom was living in a false-hearted world. How can I help her escape and find what she is in search of, that intangible hard-to-find something?

Three days later the law arrived at Blossom's house. The neighbors were unhappy with the weekly barrage of activities, music, and screams from teenage and adult guests engaging in free sex, alcohol, and drugs. All present at the gathering, including Blossom and her mom, were taken to the local jail and the legal procedures began.

⚞+ +⚟

Blossom was still searching and still reaching for the intangible.

I left the Bohemian boutique with a flower bud in hand, hoping that one day it would blossom.

SILENT KEYS

J ess dropped her backpack and sat at her desk, refusing to change into her uniform as the other students staggered in, changed, and scurried to their desks.

She slumped forward, her breaths shallow and rapid and her left arm protecting her rib cage. She flinched each time she moved, her eyes deep in darkness. I wasn't sure if it was pain or fear of what I may say, but experience told me that Jess had a fractured rib so I called her to my office.

The stone-cold office walls silenced our breath and Jess hung her head, her eyes focused on her feet. Time passed with no words.

"Would you like to tell me about this, Jess?" I asked.

"I don't remember much."

Expecting her not to want to tell me anything, I persisted. "Why don't you tell me about your home life?"

"I guess there was a time we were happy, but I don't remember that," she began. "I know Mom jumps when Dad tells her to do something, and if it's not fast enough, he hits her. And she knows it's her fault because she always says so. I get hit, too, if I don't do what he wants or if Mom doesn't apologize. My brother is just like him. I guess that's marriage and raising kids. I suppose that's a girl's place."

"Dear, dear Jess, you need out of that home," I said.

Jess didn't respond.

"Last night he smashed Mom into furniture and tossed me to the floor," she continued. "He and my brother kicked me all over."

I saw new cuts over her body and untreated old ones plus bruises and cigarette burn scars. Her head, ribs, and flank area were varying shades of black, purple, and yellow.

"My boyfriend loves me," Jess said. "He's twenty-eight and has a job at the gas station."

That she believed, but the cigarette burns were from Boyfriend's rage.

"I cause the problems. Ya know, I don't do things the way he likes them done. I washed the car wrong one time."

I wanted to hurl but dug deep for my composure. Has life shoveled this child into nothingness? I wanted Jess to feel a warm, true love. With as much gentleness as I could rally, I begged, "Let me help you."

⊨⊰⊹⊱⊨

Piles of tissues littered the floor, hiding the tears of a cold world. Jess and I trudged through the heavy snows of injustice as we made our way to the main office. My supervisor, Ms. Tost, stood at the conference room door with the Child Protective Services advocate, Mr. Dowdy. He was a narrow-chested, shaggy-bearded bald man who smelled of stale nicotine, and he leaned against the wall as if it may collapse.

Jess retold the beating. Ms. Tost pulled her glasses down on her nose and glared over the rim, her arctic eyes following me without a blink. Mr. Dowdy sat in a straight-backed chair that supported his unbending body.

Jess and I left the room for EMTs to examine her. Her breathing remained shallow and painful, and she offered a slight wave as the ambulance drove her away for further testing.

Snow blew in and the wind sent a chill through the main office as I re-entered the building.

Mr. Dowdy said, "Social workers have visited Jess's home several times and found no signs of abuse. This girl lies. Besides, she'll be eighteen in a few months."

Aging out of the system. My arm hairs stood like soldiers at attention and my head cocked to the side in anger. "You can't be serious!" I exclaimed. "This won't be our problem in a few months so you let her suffer now, when you can help? The next beating could kill her! Can you live with that on your conscience?"

Disgusting. The only response he gave was a nod and a smirk. I pictured Dowdy's ice-covered heart and looked away through my tears, but I couldn't escape envisioning Jess's life.

I stood, stiffened my body, and felt my neck veins throb and my teeth clench. My voice became louder and louder as I screamed the gist of her story. "She told you she was thrown to the floor, kicked, beaten. This child is a punching bag for their every whim." My hand slammed the table like a ship ramming an iceberg, and Ms. Tost escorted me out as I continued my tirade. "Do you care at all about Jess? What about her mother and her brother who'll just continue this cycle of hatred and abuse? No, you don't care. But wait till you see Jess's X-rays!"

If only there were an X-ray to show emotional and mental damage, I thought.

Three fractured ribs and multiple contusions. I had hope that Jess's mom cared so I phoned her. She answered, fearful and hysterical.

"You're the one who wanted this kid in the first place," I heard in the background, followed by crashing glass. "It's not my fault you didn't finish high school. Stupid bitch. I gave you an out to stay home so you could take care of me. But no, you had to have kids. You weren't happy with me. Well, I'm not happy with you, Woman. Git me another beer."

I heard a slapping—a warning of violence to come—and the phone hit the floor as Jess's mother whimpered and begged forgiveness.

I hung up and dialed 911 for the second time that day and cried an avalanche of tears alone.

I was stuffing my messenger bag and preparing to leave before the blizzard worsened when the phone rang. It was Jess's neighbor, Ms. Laney. She had driven Jess home from the hospital and Jess was spending the night with her.

Time and again Ms. Laney sheltered, fed, clothed, and protected Jess from her father and brother, and I thanked God for her.

※◄┼┼►※

There is a hope at Christmas for most children, a joy about the mystery of Santa, but make-believe ends when a child steps out of innocence into reality.

Jess was dreading the Christmas holiday. Her reality was survival—outliving name-calling, violence, and neglect and enduring the whims of her father, brother, and boyfriend. There was no hope, joy, or mystery—only cruelty. Christmas was no more than a snowman who rolled in each year and then melted away, along with her dreams for love, family, and safety.

I contacted Ms. Laney, who promised some together time with Jess—cookie-baking, tree-trimming, going to church, and ice skating.

I tried to convince myself that the next time would be easier, but I knew that was a lie.

⊷⊶

Jess had been absent thirteen consecutive days following the Christmas break when Mr. Dowdy visited her home and classified her as a runaway. I was initially concerned about more abuse, but Jess had spent most of the break with Ms. Laney.

Had she escaped an unwanted life with no purpose except to serve as an object of destruction? I could only hope.

I phoned Ms. Laney, who informed me that Jess had fled with her boyfriend two days prior. And Jess's flight actually raised her family's spirits! There was one less mouth to feed.

Neither I nor Ms. Laney ever heard from Jess again.

⊷⊶

In the 1960s, I knew little of child abuse. In the 1970s and 1980s, I kept quiet about such misery, reporting only what was required of me as a nurse. I took no further responsibility although I personally knew battered women and children. Secrets were buried to be forgotten over time. As women and children sank deeper and deeper into the abyss of abuse, my failure was not easy to accept.

I will never forget Ms. Tost's words to me.

"You are never to dial 911 from your classroom for any student or family member nor will you phone Child Protective Services ever again or I'll have your job. I determine whether or not they are to be contacted."

And I knew at that moment that I would no longer be silent.

THE FRAGILE VASE

My students had been fascinated thus far with our two-week study of psychiatric conditions, but sixty minutes into that day's lesson, depression and suicide, Natalie went to my office and sat in silence until lunch dismissal.

"I had a sister, Ashley," she said. "She was two years older than me and was the smart, pretty one. I'm the dumb, ugly daughter. She did everything right and even had the right friends. She was my parents' favorite. I can't do anything the way they want me to. They don't like me or my boyfriend and tell me I'm bad because I have a two-year old son. They won't help me take care him. And I don't think they like him either. They always wanna know why I can't be like Ashley." Natalie struggled with words between tears. "But they didn't know her. After a couple years of smokin' dope and snortin' cocaine, she overdosed at home and I found her. All they do is talk about her and how perfect she was. They don't do nothing for me. I embarrass them. I'm to blame for not getting all As. And they don't like my friends. I just want them to know I hurt too. They hate me for getting pregnant and not being married. I'm so stupid. Guess I deserve it."

I didn't know what to say.

"They even blame me for Ashley's death. I tried to get her off drugs. But she just laughed at me and told me she knew what she was doing. My mom won't believe me. She didn't believe me when I told her the first time, months before Ashley overdosed."

Weeks passed before Natalie and I spoke again. I learned that Natalie's fiancé, twenty-three-year-old Brent, attended our local college and cared for their son, Clay, while Natalie was at school.

"My mom screamed at me again last night for giving Ashley her drugs," Natalie confided. "I don't do drugs and neither does Brent. But Mom won't listen. I just want her to hug me and love me."

⊨⊰╀ ╀⊱⊨

On the last day of February, my class chose its annual service project: a school-wide health fair. Natalie, our chairperson, and her committee set to work planning the event for the first Thursday of May.

The community organizations' response was overwhelming and the class was excited. Natalie worked closely with classmates to organize tables and arrange appropriate space for each agency's displays, and Jackie scheduled students to assist agency representatives, direct clients, and serve lunches. The school secretary, Ms. Jordan, even cut fresh flowers from her private greenhouse and placed them, in vases she had hand-painted, on each of the tables.

The smallest vase caught my eye. It was miniature compared to the others and was the color of burnished bronze with crazing around the surface, giving it a fragile appearance.

Ms. Jordan spotted me as I inspected the vase.

"I am so sorry I had to use that vase," she said. "I just didn't have enough for all the tables. I want to throw it away. In fact, I will when today's over."

"Oh, please don't throw this gem away," I said. "If you don't want it, I could use it."

The class followed Natalie's calm direction as she greeted agency representatives from the local hospital, city and county health departments, family planning services, area health and fitness centers, the American Heart Association, the American Diabetes Association, and the American Red Cross.

The culinary students had prepared meals and snacks for the agency workers and had also shaped two ice sculptures: Sunshine and Vase with Flowers. The latter was a bouquet of vibrant, crinkled dried flowers curving through the ice. Tiger lilies formed an umbrella over roses, red carnations, and baby's breath, and tucked behind were goldenrod and Queen Anne's lace—soft wildflowers in a safe place that transformed as the ice melted.

Students browsed the displays, talked with presenters, and gathered pamphlets. And a parade of people from the community marched through.

Janet nudged me and whispered, "That's Natalie's mom heading our way. Look out," as she and I signed in blood donors.

Mom had taut skin with salt-and-pepper windblown hair. She wore black pants, a white blouse, and an enormous black and white checkered cape. A cigarette hung between her painted red lips.

Mom's eyes aimed directly at me as she announced, "I am Natalie's mother."

"How thrilled we are you came," I said.

She stiffened and refused to shake hands, then about-faced and walked down the hallway in search of her daughter.

"Natalie is a wonderful student with so much ability," I said, keeping stride with her. "She organized today's events under my guidance. Her classmates love her and she has gained their support in this. You should be quite proud."

Checkered-caped mom ignored me and my comments, then blew smoke in my face and flicked her cigarette to the floor. Within seconds she unleashed vile wrath upon me, putting both hands on her hips and leaning into me.

"Who do you think you are, some Goody Two-shoes? You're revolting...none of your business...sue you...Natalie's a doper, a loser, hopeless."

All nearby heard her.

Natalie arrived and Mom turned to her with a cascade of destructive words.

"You little tramp...no good...you should be home with Clay...no, that no-good Brent is...I'll get custody. That'll show you. You slut...too bad Ashley isn't here to straighten you out...you're comin' with me."

Her lengthy, loud speech dehumanized Natalie. Words scathed the administrator on duty. Mom wanted Natalie home, at once. I couldn't fathom why.

"I don't understand," I said. "This is a proud moment being overshadowed by your condemnation—Natalie's success lost by criticism and your love replaced with bitterness."

Natalie looked down, her shoulders slumping as tears formed.

"You cause problems with what you do here," her mom lashed at me. "She should be home with her son. And my relationship with Natalie is none of your business. And don't you dare judge me either. You think you know everything."

Natalie's mother swelled with rage and hatred as others looked on in horror. Mom snared Natalie and steered her away by the elbow.

I couldn't shake Natalie's mother's acid words from my thoughts. Does she think I attempted to unravel her relationship with Natalie? It is not easy to raise children and she had already lost one daughter. But one remained.

I phoned Natalie's mom but there was no answer. I just wanted to say, "Hold tight to your delicate, fragile daughter."

Time slipped away, month by month, until another Christmas arrived. It was a difficult Christmas for Natalie. Her parents had kicked her out of their home and Brent didn't have enough income for housing and all of Clay's needs plus his own college education. So Natalie and three-year-old Clay moved into a visitor's room above a church sanctuary. Brent paid for their needs and helped care for Clay so Natalie could continue her high school education.

I rose as the day dawned. It was Natalie's high school graduation day and she had grants for college.

A cool spring breeze ruffled my hair, and I noticed the wild-flowers at the edge of a thicket near the school. I picked a small bouquet and placed it in my cracked, fragile vase for Natalie—a reminder of the beauty that is hers, a fragile beauty that can transform even the darkest, fractured days.

OBLIVIOUS

Matted braids with bits of embedded slime and mud framed Emma's sunbaked face as her puffy, dark-circled eyes stared at me from her desk. As I approached her I heard gasps and wheezing followed by moist coughing.

"Emma, sit up straight please," I said. "Do you have your inhaler?"

"I forgot it," she said in slow labored speech. "Didn't take my medicine either."

I sat facing her. "Emma, look at me. Breathe with me. Pause. In. Out. In. Out."

"My chest hurts," she said.

Dustin phoned the office and asked Debbie, the secretary, to call Emma's mom.

Emma squeaked, "Mom worked night turn. She's sleeping. Don't call."

There was no answer anyway.

I wheeled Emma to the office and left her in the safety of three women—two secretaries and the principal. Keeping her calm was all we could do.

After school I walked briskly to catch Debbie, noting three staff members with aerosol cans in hand. The office smelled like a perfume counter at the local mall.

"Emma left on the school bus. She's so heavy she could barely lift her legs up the bus steps. And we do not appreciate babysitting her," Debbie said. "Doesn't she ever wash her clothes or bathe? She smells of days-old sweat and now the entire office stinks of soured milk, fermented laundry, stale urine, cabbage, and fish."

I dodged aerosol sprays as I ambled to my lab, my lip and nose curling upward in disgust at their complete disregard for and obliviousness to Emma's plight.

I phoned Emma's mom, Mabel, in hopes of deciphering just exactly what Emma's circumstances were.

"My husband works at Country Market," she told me. "He cleans, stocks, and repairs stuff. The owner's a good man to keep him on. And I work as a companion to a man with cerebral palsy who needs someone with him at night."

"I admire you both," I said, genuinely.

"Emma had another episode on the bus," Mabel continued with a softness in her voice, "but we can't afford her medicine without health coverage. She'll have to learn to do without. I told the doc. Thanks for not sending her to the hospital. We can't afford the ambulance fee."

"Asthma is a serious condition but is manageable with—"

She cut me off. All her children were home from school. I heard their voices clamoring around her.

Two days later Emma returned to school. I taught her proper care for asthma and about potential complications, but I struggled to get through to her on proper hygiene.

My colleague, Diane, and I gave her soap, feminine wipes, shampoo, conditioner, deodorant, and nail clippers. I washed her clothes and we gave her laundry detergent. But the sour milk, fermented laundry, stale urine, cabbage, and fish smells remained.

Emma had become my shadow, and, since all else had failed, I bought an aerosol.

Emma's grades also suffered because she lacked focus. She had run-ins with teachers over failure to complete or turn in assignments regularly.

A month later Emma began chattering loudly, jumping out of her seat, and pacing while class was in session. She wiped her brow and flailed her hands. Her face was flushed, her breathing was rapid, and her pulse was racing and irregular.

"Emma, have you taken any illegal drugs this morning?" I asked.

"I just smoke cigarettes," she said. "Last night my parents took me to the ER. The doc there gave me some new medicine. I couldn't sleep last night, my head hurts now, and my arms and legs feel like a pin is pricking them."

I dialed 911. By the time Emma reached the hospital, she required oxygen, her muscles were twitching, and she had developed tachycardia from the medication reaction.

Emma had no way home from the hospital so I taxied her. She directed me to a forsaken mobile home park in the backwater part of the countryside. I remained silent, my observations poignant reminders of lives not usually seen. The destitute pulled curtains aside as I drove by and then closed them hastily so I didn't notice them. I continued with caution, meandering through stupor and rejection to the end of the street.

The mobile home, nestled between a rusty, run-down pickup truck and a ramshackle fence, looked like an abandoned outbuilding. A ghost-white, gaunt Mabel with darkness circling her eyes greeted me at the doorway. She impressed me as intense and worn from life. I met Emma's five brothers and sisters: Emmett, Ezra, Ethan, Shay, and Summer. The family of eight shared two bedrooms, three bunks, and one bathroom—the whole place the size of a burial vault. The impressive combination of spaghetti, cigarette smoke, garlic, and stale urine lingered in my nose, and I felt an unforgivable oblivion of poverty.

⸻

"Today we will discuss Maslow's hierarchy of needs from *A Theory of Human Motivation*," I announced.

Keyshawn drew the pyramid on our new whiteboard.

"Step 1: Basic physiological needs must be met for survival," I began.

Emma was unable to breathe.

"Step 2: Safety and survival is argued as the primary need for growth."

Emma smoked despite suffering from asthma and had no money for medication.

What else can they not afford? I wondered.

I carried on, though I became increasingly aware of the practical application to my student's life.

"Step 3: Love and belonging"

Did Emma feel accepted? She said she had no time for friends.

"Step 4: Esteem"

Would Emma master knowledge and skills? She said she didn't have any. Would she attain personal goals? She said she had none.

"Step 5: Self-actualization"

Would Emma ever pursue her moral ideals and creativity, reach her potential, or find joy in life?

⸻

Emma arrived with vertical scratches on her lower left leg. Cat? Raccoon? Her leg was red and swollen and pus oozed from it.

Emma said, "I fell through a hole in the floor at home. I forgot it hid under the rug."

That rug lay there a month ago and I had been oblivious.

Later that same day Emma's parents arrived for a conference and my colleagues left the room, propping the door open. Mabel hugged me, and I shook Bob's sandpapery hand. I sensed stale cigarettes, onion, fish, and sweat. Bob spoke in a hoarse voice and his unwashed gray beard spread across his face without direction. His wrinkle-crowded smile revealed crooked yellow teeth and tobacco nuggets.

Survival. The struggling deprived. There was no plan for Emma's future. Their reality was alternative to mine. We discussed their home, medical problems, the hole in the floor, and six children rather than the upcoming internships. Their land was used to raise crops for harvest and canning. I listened as the hazy grime of poverty wrapped around me and the stench of the deprived engulfed me. An hour later, they departed. I washed my hands and had a new appreciation for fresh air.

When internship time arrived, I placed Emma at the city health department. I knew the staff and explained her situation, and they agreed to help. Internships only lasted two weeks.

Two days into her rotation, Peg, Emma's mentor and my dear friend, phoned.

"The staff will no longer tolerate her odor," she said. "The health department's patients are complaining. Room fresheners and open windows are completely ineffective."

I explained my past efforts and experiences. Peg changed heart and assigned Emma to organizing files in a back room. Peg taught her hygiene via demonstrations and gave Emma supplies.

Emma lasted three more days before I pulled her from the site at Peg's request. Emma spent her remaining internship time with me in the lab. I stressed deodorant, retaught hygiene, opened doors and windows, and sprayed aerosol—but Emma remained oblivious to it all.

THAT'S THE WAY IT IS

Marnie helped me arrange surgical instruments, sterile wraps and dressings, and tape and bandages while she waited for Addie to pick her up.

At first Marnie talked about her life in California but then she blurted out, "I'm a cutter. Have been for a while. I get so miserable and it's the only way I feel better."

She rolled up her sleeves. Both arms displayed short and long and deep and shallow cuts that layered the skin in a mass of crisscross overlaps.

"Addie, that's my mom, she don't care I call her that. She drinks too much. Hangs 'round the local bars and night-clubs. Men bring her home to spend the night."

We stopped preparation for the next day's lesson and sat at a lab table. Her story began at the age of ten.

"My sister, Jenn, and I used to do Saturday chores with Addie. Anyway, everything was fun. John, my dad, was great. He chased us around the yard, played ball with us. Jenn liked to play tea party, so Dad and I sat on a pillowed floor and drank pretend tea. After the chores were done, he'd take Jenn and me fishin'. Then one day Dad left and never came back. He never gave me a kiss goodbye and didn't hug Jenn. How could he? I barely remember him now. Sometime after he left a neighbor reported men comin' and goin'. I saw people take Addie away. And Jenn and I went to separate foster homes. We cried 'cause Mom was all we had left. Grammi died right after Dad left. Addie did come back in about six months. I hated livin' in somebody else's house."

"That's something I can't imagine, Marnie," I said.

"Jenn won't help me do chores anymore. I gotta clean, cook, pack our lunches, wash dishes, and wash the clothes. Addie doesn't even buy our food. I have to do that. There's no time for playin' softball and Addie wouldn't sign the forms anyway. I wish Dad hadn't left. And I love science, but you know that. Dad and I built rockets and made a weather vane. We made a volcano once and the lava covered the entire kitchen table. Addie even laughed. We planted a flower garden together and Dad, Jenn, and me had a vegetable garden too. We loved to eat the tomatoes right there in the garden, dirt and all."

I smiled as she finished the candy bar and grapes I'd given her, and I handed her a bottle of water.

"I tried to protect my sister. I hid her and screamed and hit them. Addie pretended she never heard but I'm not so sure she cared. So the men took it out on me and then they found Jenn. I couldn't keep her safe. She cuts too."

"You are both so young to be in that type of environment," I said.

"It's been that way so long. Ya get used to it. Mom's always drinkin' and that's how it happens. She passes out and the men, well...after I fight them they still rape me, and when they found Jenn, they made her watch me get raped. Later I held her and we cried together. Mom came in and threw a bottle of booze at us 'cause we disturbed her and some man."

"Is that how you got the scar on your forehead?" I asked.

"Yes."

Two hours had passed and a soft snow was tumbling down. Addie's arrival looked bleak. The last bus had left and school personnel had departed an hour ago. And Jenn waited at her school, too, on an unreachable Addie.

"Marnie, what's for dinner? I'm starved," Jenn said when we picked her up.

I pulled into a fast-food spot and bought burgers with the works plus extras and then drove them to their small two-bedroom apartment. Lights on behind the closed curtains of other apartments created a soft velvety glow across the snow.

Addie was nowhere—no note to her daughters, no words of love.

Jenn stormed off to a bedroom and shut the door with a solid thud, a warning to keep out. Marnie called several of Addie's hangouts and located her mother at Jack's Bar and Grill. A friend planned to bring her home later.

Marnie told me, "It'll be the wee hours of the morning. Most nights turn out this way. Once I get my license I'll go and get her."

"Do you think that's too late to be out on a school night?" I asked.

"Oh well, that's the way it is."

I wrote Addie a note. "I drove Marnie and Jenn home from school this evening. It was getting late and I was concerned about the roads. All is well. Marnie is a wonderful young lady and a bright student. She has a lot to look forward to. And Jenn seems like a delightful young girl. Please feel free to call me at the school."

I left my card with my office phone number for Addie and gave my home number to Marnie in case she ever needed it. I trudged to the car noticing that our previous footprints had already been erased.

Late one evening my phone rang. The caller spoke slurred words.

"Do not interfere again. I will take care of Marnie and Jenn."

I heard glasses clink in the background.

"Give me another round."

Then I picked up loud music and men's voices.

"I drove them home to be sure they were safe," I said.

I felt a cold chill radiate through my body as ice too thick to thaw formed between Addie and me.

⟫⊹⊹⟪

Three days later when the snowstorm had passed and roads were safe, school resumed.

Marnie appeared at my office doorway. I'd seen her look before—a hollow misery, a silent tunnel within the soul that freezes the heart.

"Last night they raped Jenn. I couldn't stop them," she cried.

Tears unstoppable. I looked at Marnie. She had so much to give, yet more had been taken from her and from Jenn than I would ever understand. I prayed for the right words.

"Marnie, you and Jenn have each other as dear friends. And you know you always have God with you too."

Marnie spoke among the sobs. "My Grammi always told me that. She always read her Bible and read it to me and Jenn too."

⟫⊹⊹⟪

Little changed over the winter and into spring. Child Protective Services found nothing unsuitable or improper in the home, simply a single mother who struggled to raise two teenage girls. Marnie and Jenn told no one else what went on behind closed doors at home. Marnie continued to spend time with me after school, coming alone in her pain, while Addie relished the bar scene and Jenn began to mimic Addie's life.

STRUGGLES

"It's like a big electric jolt racing through my whole body; it jerks and I have no control of it," Alan told me. "It's like when somebody's trying to go to sleep and their foot twitches—so embarrassing and really awful. I used to call them fits but now I know better."

"How do you handle your seizures, Alan?" I asked.

"Well, my mom doesn't want me to have accidents, so she buys me plastic cups with lids and all my dishes 'n silverware's plastic. That way if I jerk, I won't hurt myself. If I go somewhere, I take my own stuff with me. You know, I fall to the floor if I'm standing. I've hit the back of my head before and had a goose egg."

"Do you take medication?" I asked.

"When I need it. The doctor said it's epilepsy, but Mom and Dad say it's just part of me, like who I am."

"And what do you think?"

Unfazed, he shrugged.

"You never talked to your parents about the medication?" I prodded.

"There's nothing to say, really. The doctor said I need to take the meds as he directed and to get in touch with him if I have a seizure. But Mom and Dad don't bother to call. Honestly, I don't think they can afford to buy my meds." His too-long curly black hair fell about his face as he lowered his head. "Dad was laid off from his job at the plant and Mom only works for minimum wage. After they started a family, they couldn't afford for Mom to finish college."

"Alan, what if I investigate some methods to help pay for these medications? And then you could inform your parents?"

"You'd do that?" he asked, peering through his locks appreciatively.

Within a week the school counselor and I had found an epilepsy foundation willing to help. But a few days later my supervisor visited me.

"Leave this alone," the supervisor said. "You only cause problems and increase my workload when you interfere in students' lives. You enable them. It's better not to know or ask questions."

If he hadn't walked out the door, I would have kindly corrected him on all counts rather than defending my actions aloud to myself.

"Alan came to me," I said. "His having a healthy, productive life is at stake. Alan cannot learn if he is not healthy. I see my role as one to educate and protect our students, and I'm doing just that by providing the means to obtain something: enabling, yes."

I gave an excited Alan the foundation's information for his parents. He smiled and thanked me.

But on Monday I could tell from the look on his face and in his tired black eyes that the information had not been well-received, especially by Alan's father. Alan's hope was all but destroyed.

My heart sank for him. How can I help his parents understand that Alan's epilepsy deserves their immediate attention and get them to trust and follow doctor's orders when perhaps they have never done so before?

Later that day Alan's mom phoned me.

"I'm drowning," she said. "I'm confused and in pain. Alan needs help and Harry, Alan's dad, is out of control and depressed."

There was more happening in Alan's life than he had shared with me.

For a week I mulled over everything I had learned about Alan and his family. Then I phoned Harry.

He answered in a gruff voice with a thick, burly speech and I introduced myself.

He commanded, "Don't waste your time with busy words, lady."

But my words came in rapid succession. "Sir, Alan has frequent seizures and says he takes his medication sporadically. He struggles in his schoolwork with tests and skill performance that is perhaps caused by his poor vision. Alan reads at a fifth-grade level and math is just as difficult for him. I would like to schedule Alan for testing so the school can provide special help if he qualifies. Also, there is a foundation that will help pay for Alan's epilepsy medication."

"Alan is a whiz kid. Not one thing wrong with that young man," Harry retorted, implying that I was mistaken and that I had his wife and Alan thinking all wrong.

I stumbled over my words. "Harry, I just want you to know that I'm trying to help Alan like I know you want to."

Silence lingered. Then, in a softer voice, he said, "My life's been a series of bad decisions. I was in college for chemistry when Ilene an' I fell in love an' got married. She got pregnant and dropped out of school, so there went her dance career. After Alan was born, I quit college too. Our parents wouldn't help us." Sorrow filled his voice. "I drank more and more until I landed in a forgotten world. Tried to quit lots of times, but when somethin' goes wrong, I start all over again. Do whatever you can for Alan," he said and hung up.

I enjoyed the silence, knowing that Alan would receive the help he needed. But if hope never has freedom to expand, does it become purely wishful thinking? I wondered.

SHOVELS AND BROOMS

Gray puffy clouds hung high in the sky dropped a light snow and gave rise to a lingering gloom as Chrissy's and Jake's classmates and I arrived at the funeral home that afternoon.

Jake found a chair away from family, where Chrissy joined him after placing a book in her mother's casket. Controlled grief consumed the family. They had done this before when Chrissy and Jake's father had died five years ago.

⊨⊰⊹⊱⊨

Blisters on Chrissy's hands, bruises on her legs, and gashes on her arms pointed to diseased behavior evolving in the months following Chrissy and Jake's loss.

Chrissy wore sunglasses and draped her unwashed hair over her spirited brown eyes. This once-manicured girl now wore wrinkled, mismatched clothes and muddy shoes. Her uniforms had rings of dried mud on the hems and stains on the tops. Chrissy argued with me and her classmates, and Jake's lab instructor, Mr. Lucas, told me that Jake was absent at least two days a week.

During lunch one day I heard screams and furniture screeching on the cafeteria's tile floor. Then I was summoned to the conference room.

Chrissy and Jake sat at opposite ends of the table. A two-inch gash above his right eye had created a bright red waterfall down his face. Chrissy had one welt on her upper left arm and another on her chest. She leaned forward into a wad of tissues to trap the blood pumping from her nose. And Jake took a deep breath, glaring at Chrissy. His tensed muscles reminded me of a statue.

I sat beside Jake and placed a firm hand of quiet authority on his arm. Mr. Lucas and the supervisor, Mrs. Dylan, walked in. And the teacher on lunch duty, Mr. Marker, arrived, his shirt arm torn.

Mrs. Dylan placed a hand on her hip and glared heartlessly over her glasses.

"The punishment for lunchroom fights is a five-day suspension, including a failing grade in each class for the duration of those five days," she announced.

Discipline that worked with one student almost never worked with another.

"Perhaps rather than suspending them and destroying their grades they could help the custodians," I suggested. "It would lighten the workload a bit and Chrissy and Jake could work off some of their hostility and maybe even begin to function together."

My idea was shot down immediately.

Chrissy clenched her lips as she filled with rage, and Jake curled his fingers tightly around a pencil until it snapped. I gripped his fist but he jerked it away and whirled his head toward me. I knew then that the cancer would spread, dark and deep.

Later that day I had a not-so-cooperative conversation with Chrissy.

"Chrissy, is there a reason you fight so much with Jake?"

She pursed her lips, then spoke. "He's a jerk."

"In your eyes, yes, but don't you think he's hurting? I mean, just losing his mother and having no father? And you, too, are hurting, if you're honest with yourself."

"You know nothing," she growled.

Several days later I contacted her older brother, Matt.

"Her behavior is none of my concern," he said, adamantly refusing to talk with me. "I have my own family to consider."

I understood his position and phoned Chrissy's older sister, Tristan. She shared my concerns about her siblings, but her words were bitter.

"I have no control over those two rebels," Tristan said. "I will not have them in my life full time. I will not help them, adopt them, or move in with them. It is not an option. And don't call Matt again about this matter."

"What would you like me to do for them? What can we do for them?" I asked, but she hung up.

I waited two days and phoned her again. Hours later Tristan arrived at my office, her long straight black hair shining under the fluorescent lights. There was a softness in her high cheekbones that accented her deep-set eyes. I treaded lightly around her mother's death and Chrissy's grades and overall behavior, sensing she was more beautiful before wounds and grief had masked her.

Tristan tapped her fingertips on the chair arm. "Would you get to the point? I don't have all afternoon."

I told Tristan about Chrissy and Jake's fight.

"They'll just have to work it out themselves," she said nonchalantly.

"And what about a legal guardian for Chrissy?" I asked.

"Look, Jake is eighteen. He is the adult in Chrissy's life. That makes him her legal guardian."

"Do you think that's in her best interest?" I pressed.

"I might as well tell you because you're not going to stop interfering in Chrissy's life. Jake is unpredictable. He camps in a shed behind the house. All he does is work on engines: four-wheelers, lawn mowers, and pickups. Chrissy stays in the house and cleans and cooks. After Dad passed, she cared for Mom. Mom couldn't walk because of an old back injury, so she sat in a wheelchair all day. I watched Mom cry all the time, then withdraw from us. Giving up her own needs, Chrissy imitated a nursemaid and I moved out."

"What can we do to help them?" I pleaded.

"You can't do anything and I'm not. Jake loses himself in machines, draining fluids and removing the very heart of an engine. Chrissy rummages through the house, scrubbing with a vengeance until the house is snowy white and unblemished. Why should any of us solve their problems?"

"It's been difficult on both of them. Don't you think they struggle?" I asked, seeking compassion.

"I know what you think. I should raise them, be the adult in their lives. Look, I'm getting married in four months. I can't take them. I won't take them. They are out of control, and, like I said, Jake is eighteen."

"But what about your older brother, Matt?"

"He's our half-brother who escaped when he was sixteen. I guess he got tired of defending the three of us. He'd taken enough knocks of his own," Tristan said bitterly, stiffening in her seat. "Dad beat all four of us."

Bitterness returned in her silence.

"Dad swung a shovel at Chrissy, so she grabbed a broom and swung back, smacking him in the face." Tristan took a deep breath. "He came back at her and chased her around the porch, down the steps, and out into the yard. Dad brought that shovel down across her back, knocking her to the ground. We all thought he was going to hit her again when he raised the shovel. And that's when Matt stepped in and slugged him in the jaw."

My mind drifted to intangible fragments of anger and violence. It wasn't the physically punishing hits on the back, bloodied and fractured noses, or broken teeth and bruised cheeks. It wasn't the heat of anger and rage. No, it was the freezing fear and lack of trust in others. It was the defiance, intense self-control, and deep-seated anger that remained as unknown consequential scars.

"That was the last time he stood up for any of us," Tristan continued. "It was the last time I saw Matt. He did not even come to their funerals. I guess I understand. I mean, Mom just watched and never did a thing to help us. We kept it all a secret."

"We have to think about Chrissy and Jake," I persisted.

"They're both like Dad. The fight you told me about happened because Jake tracked mud into the house. Chrissy had just scrubbed the floor. She chased him outside with the mop, and he hit her with a shovel he had left in the yard. They brought the fight here with them, I guess. I've learned it's a cycle of power, rage, and control. I told you, I'm not raising them. They'll just have to work it out themselves."

⤙⧗⤚

Four months later I sat in the corner of my favorite coffee shop, burying myself in the next day's class preparation. My thoughts wandered to the hostility and violence in Chrissy and Jake's family. It's rather like my coffee—bitter and drawing me in for more.

As a man and woman drew closer, I was surprised to see Tristan. She introduced me to her brother, Matt. They had recently reconnected and wanted to help Chrissy and Jake.

"I started taking my family to church again, the same one Mom used to take us to when she could," Matt said. "I always liked the priest there and my kids seem to like him too. Maybe Jake would go with me if I asked."

"That is a great idea," I said. "What about you, Tristan? Would you be willing to ask Chrissy to go with you?"

Tristan sighed and said, "I suppose. I just wasn't into that stuff."

"Tristan, we said we'd do what we could and that you can do smiling," Matt said.

"You know, this could be a great beginning with your brother and sister," I said, hopeful. "Matt, you might try showing interest in Jake's mechanical work and how he wants to pursue his dreams. And Tristan, Chrissy really wants to get into nursing and loves to cook. Maybe you could have her fix dinner for you and let her talk about her goals in life. Chrissy and Jake are really wonderful young individuals. They are both intelligent and hardworking. Their classmates like them and look to them for leadership. Please don't give up on them, even though they can both be stubborn."

They laughed quietly in hopes of a tender reunion.

When I left two hours later, having gotten little done in preparation for the next day's class, I thought of Kalen and his keys.

PART TWO

a time to kill, and a time to heal;
a time to break down, and a time to build up…

Ecclesiastes 3:3 ESV

UNENDING STREETS

Professor Rawson, known as Santa on campus, had made this appointment with me a week ago. He turned to face the window as I entered his Westgate State University office a captive audience of one.

He spoke in a slow, articulate fashion. "Have a seat. Your supervisor and principal have asked me to talk with you about your teaching practices. They sense you are zealous in your pursuit to educate and guide students. You want to improve their lives, give them a chance at a good future, I'm sure."

"Of course."

He continued his cadence, looking over the top of his glasses perched low on his nose. "Well, your administration has asked me to provide an authentic learning experience for you, one to broaden your horizons and, most importantly, help you grasp theories of education without enabling your students."

My learning experience was scheduled for three days later.

I crossed a bridge over the interstate and the real estate changed from the steel mills and the campus to immigrant housing from the

Industrial Revolution. Three-to-five-story high dilapidated buildings and homes with broken and boarded-up windows, doors off
hinges, peeling paint, and holey roofs lined the streets. Men cruised
and women loitered in scanty attire, and shabby people with bags
and grocery carts hung out between buildings on the dark side
streets, hiding from the music and noise that saturated the air.

My directions took me down a side street to the third house on
the left. The driveway was a thin layer of gravel with weeds inter-
twining in a large hump in the center. The garage was a detached
cement block building with two cars, an old rusty lawn mower,
and other equipment inside. Flakes of cream paint sprinkled the
ground. Above the house entrance was a tattered hand-painted
sign: SUNRISE. It hung at a diagonal with one nail missing.

I remained in my van, weighing the value of Professor Rawson's
thoughts and my administration's request against my personal
experience.

My students were sixteen-to-eighteen-years-old and deserved
respect. And I expected them to respect me, my judgement, and
our program and school. My relationship with them was well-estab-
lished. In my two years of teaching I had not only seen students
graduate with honors and head to college but do so with scholarships—scholarships we had searched for together. Yet my supervisor and principal wanted me to experience SUNRISE.

I did not use education theory to educate. I applied nursing
theory and practice: protecting students from harm, advocating
for them, and defending what was right. Assess, plan, intervene,
evaluate, and reteach was the plan. It was professional and there
were results.

Enable? Yes. I built strength in each student so they could
endure and improve weaknesses. I empowered and prepared them
for their futures while allowing each to develop personal abilities.
Most students left my classroom with their heads held high, joy in
their achievements, and the courage to chase their dreams.

The ten wooden steps to the back door creaked and shifted. I grasped the loose, slimy doorknob and entered the kitchen. A man sat on a counter stool smoking a cigarette and a woman in blue jeans and a tight-fitting T-shirt introduced herself as Phyllis as she prepared a meat and cheese tray for lunch.

Phyllis led me to the pea-green dining area where the teens gathered at an oval table by a synthesizer. The dinnerware was chipped and mismatched, spoons were twisted, and forks were minus teeth. The youth grabbed the meat, cheese, buns, chips, soda, and juice. There was little interaction.

As she showed me the house, Phyllis told me about some of the young residents.

Ace played music on the synthesizer and wouldn't even look in my direction. The day prior he had attacked another student in the shelter and put him in the hospital. Another unnamed youth had beaten his brother into a coma over a dinner roll.

Keisha paced in front of the living room fireplace. The yellow brick hearth lay in ruin, blackened ash littering the grate. Cobwebs forged bridges from wall to wall. One frayed loveseat and one under-stuffed oversize chair covered with a ragged throw sat lopsided and low to the floor. Gray threadbare carpet and dingy walls, perforated by holes and marked with dark hand-drawn pictures, surrounded us.

In the main office a worn desk and chair sat in the right corner and a rotary phone sat on a small chipped table in front of the desk. One youth phone call each week was permitted with good behavior.

The staff counselor joined me on the tour as Ray approached us with his hands balled into fists, talking at me in seamless thoughts.

Placed about the basement classroom's cement floors and cracked concrete block walls were bookshelves and twelve run-down desks plus a teacher's desk. Posters and projects were not visible, I assumed, due to limited space. Odors of swampy vegetation and dirt from a tomb dampened the air and body odor lingered.

Mr. Jones, a male in his late twenties, was at the teacher's desk.

"I teach all required subjects to the students I'm handed," he said. "Usually they move in and out within two or three weeks, and every six weeks I have a completely different group of teens in crisis uninterested in learning. It's difficult for them to focus on schoolwork. And they're so behind it's hard to know what to teach. There is no proficiency or achievement testing before they go back to their assigned schools, and most return."

I observed student-teacher interaction for an hour. Cain spoke out of turn. Blade interrupted. Others garbled inarticulate, incoherent, taunting words. They called each other names and cursed the work, the food, and life. They saw no reason to live, much less learn. Crisis was their school, survival their language.

I pictured Professor Rawson tapping his pipe in the ashtray and grinning out of the corner of his mouth as he had when I received this assignment. Why did he assign me to this youth shelter? These misplaced youths are not my students, I thought. Or am I to see where some of my students might be without help?

The third floor was the girls' sleeping area. Four-to-six beds covered with thin, tattered blankets, were in each of the two rooms. One youth slept still at noon. A breeze from a broken windowpane ruffled the thin, holey, mismatched curtains. Comfort stayed out of reach there.

The young faces remained expressionless with no glow for a future, and their eyes hid memories behind glassy, distant stares. Nakita cleared the table, scowling at me. Raven sat in her fixed stare, talking to someone not visible.

These youths were there by a combination of their own choices and their circumstances. They were street youths, gang members, victims, and juvenile delinquents. When not living there, they ate garbage, found food kitchens, and slept in storm sewers and under overpasses. I wondered about their parents.

A wave of reality washed over me. There is a dire need to intervene *early* in these teens lives to ensure they are cared for. They need a way to learn life and work skills to ensure a better future for them. My vision fits right in: help my students build better lives. Administration wanted me to help the students, maintain my persistence, jump the hurdles, and prevent the students from reaching a crisis stage.

On the way home I stopped at a quiet, out-of-the-way coffee shop. I sat for a while, lost in my thoughts, isolated from humanity, and distracted by hopelessness. I whispered, "How are these youths to find their way without help?" But the statement got lost in the chaotic chorus of my heart hovering over all the day's sights, sounds, and thoughts.

There was a stench of torment beyond imagination in the reality I'd just faced. Those were the hours and places where grief lives, fear flourishes, and the truth lies. Hope and joy hide from those children. Days begin and end in silence. Their choices and circumstances create the world where they live in distinct buildings, separate spaces, and hallways of unending streets.

WEAKNESSES

Piper made her routine grand entrance. She was an energetic, blond, tall, slender young lady. Ballet lessons had given her the strength and gracefulness to strut like a peacock, her regal stride with an unassuming glide. Ginger was a redhead and five inches shorter than Piper. Nicknamed Taz for her aggressiveness on the ballfield, Ginger played shortstop for her high school's softball team.

Both girls were outspoken class leaders, addressing concerns in calm, nonconfrontational ways. At the beginning of the year, they had been inseparable friends but the class atmosphere changed one day.

Class began with book presentations. Up first was Ginger, but she didn't move.

With twenty-three young women and two young men, some days were unpleasant with cold remarks, dirty looks, accidental bumps, and gossip. This was one of those days.

Resistance within the class grew and friction intensified.

"Whatever is going on, you need to discuss this as adults," I announced confidently. But each student harbored so much personal anger that they weren't going to hear a word I said.

In unison they all stood, stomped to an open part of the lab, divided themselves into two regiments, and circled one another to form battle lines. They marked their territory.

I was clueless and situated myself between them as a mediator—or perhaps referee—while Troy and Dustin stood by the door.

What do they know that I do not? I wondered as I retreated.

Piper and Ginger threw scorching words at each other, and each of the other girls shot her own verbal arrows.

What is this about? I wondered, but neither of them ever told me and none of their classmates gave them up.

"Liar. Slut. Loser. SOB. Freakin' louse. Traitor. Thief. Fart knocker. Talk to the hand."

Hurt pierced the room like targeted radioactive waves. The look in each target's eyes when the mark was hit was unmistakable.

Such irreverence, perversion, and contempt for each other! How can my classroom ever be the same after this? I had lost control. I needed a classroom management manual.

I marched over to my large-print poster of classroom rules and read them aloud. "Respect each other. Value others' opinions, even when different from your own. Build trusting relationships. Conduct self with dignity. Demonstrate compassion."

Every rule had been desecrated. I didn't know what to do.

A colleague and friend, Daryl, whose classroom was a few doors away, entered the lab for damage control. Embarrassment was written across my forehead.

And then my supervisor rushed in, shouting, "Stop this chaos."

My students were blind to him and his words, and the battle raged on around us. I walked into the hallway with my supervisor.

"All is well. This will soon end," I reassured him.

His words nearly shattered my eardrum. "It had better stop now."

The students' voices shook the walls. Soon another instructor and supervisor heard the yelling and raced over. Troy and Dustin dealt with them. Humiliation flashed like a neon sign across my face. My teaching abilities will definitely be called into question over this debacle, I realized.

Suddenly the room fell quiet and the students returned to their seats. I rendered no solution, declared no verdict, and doled out no punishment. It was a defining moment, a defining day.

In the short time remaining, presentations were given, beginning with Ginger. The students smiled and focused, listening and asking some outstanding questions. Piper received the same response.

"Thanks for letting us talk this out," Piper said as she and Ginger headed to lunch together. "No other teacher would do that. You're the best. This thing was gonna be a full-blown fight if we hadn't done this. We're cool now."

Exhaustion set in from my not-so-stellar moments that crumbled day. I escorted myself to the administrative office, smoothed out the wrinkles in my uniform, and straightened my stance.

The superintendent was tense and livid, his outraged words crushing any discussion we might have. My weaknesses highlighted his every word: poor management, lack of discipline, no respect, and enabling. I disagreed with him on the respect and enabling issues, but I knew better than to speak. So I nodded in agreement, listening to his perspective.

⊸⊱⊰⊷

At home I brewed a fresh pot of coffee and headed to my favorite chair to grade papers, but my mind just wandered over the pages. I put the work aside and picked up the book I had been reading. It was about George Washington crossing the Delaware and forging a new path. And I was reminded how these girls wrote a piece of history with their words and all that passed between them.

Their devotion to drama was not my genre, yet my weaknesses had let them proceed. There was no editing. Had I stopped them it would have been as though I had closed the book before the end or rerouted history before it was made.

SILK PAPER

"Today I am reminded of a caterpillar's transformation into a butterfly, befitting this time of new beginnings," I began, speaking to the students and parents attending the pre-graduation luncheon celebration. "Two years ago you came to this school safe in the wrap of your cocoon—a cocoon of knowledge and experiences. We accepted you, supported you, and added to your cocoon. We guided your learning, enriched your experiences, and cultivated your heart's ambition." I paused to take in the smiling faces. "You bonded with classmates and instructors. We formed a family, recognizing your capabilities. We witnessed you adopt patience, trust, and compassion. Your transformation was messy and uncomfortable. On certain days life seemed hopeless, problems unsolvable, and your goals unpromising." I noticed a few damp eyes. "In a few days you will shed your cocoon and transform into the butterfly you are meant to be with wings as delicate as silk paper. You know your potential and have set goals. Life will get messy along the way, but you are to emerge with nectar for strength, a will to succeed, and your potential to build a better world. Stretch your wings. Flutter away as quickly as you appeared. Take hope with you, but leave behind your imprint on our hearts."

Diane, the dental instructor, introduced the parents, and Cathy, the medical secretary instructor, presented awards. Then the room slowly emptied and we were left with transient memories of each student. That was how it was each May.

⚔

Harper and I began our conversations one year ago. Early in the month of May, during my brief lunch break, Harper sat with me and ate. She alternated salads, yogurt, cottage cheese with fruit, and vegetable soup. She drank water. Some days she devoured every bite. Other days she made circles in her lunch with the plasticware.

"You know, I'm a sham," Harper blurted out one day. I wear bling-bling, but I'm sure not shining on the inside. What a phony. I've been trying to change my appearance—lose weight. Weighed myself this morning. It showed me nine pounds lighter. It's taken me four months. Like, I don't want to eat skinny food anymore. I'm really fat. I sneak candy bars at home and chips in the lunch room. And the scent of food cooking—french fries and cake and cookies—takes my willpower away. I can't ignore the smell. I eat them. All. Every bite. That's why I eat lunch with you, why I don't go to the lunch room where skinny girls eat whatever they want and flirt with the boys."

"Do you think your diet is wise?" I asked.

Harper looked at me in disgust.

"Look at me. Five-foot-nine and 225 pounds. I'm called fluffy, chubby, tubby, and el plumpo. Always have been, even by my family. Those words hurt. So I eat more. My mom tells me I'm just stocky. But I'm not stupid. I can see in the mirror."

"Are you made fun of during our lab?" I asked.

The corners of her mouth curled upward.

"Oh no. They are all nice to me. But I know they feel sorry for me. I never go out with friends or have a date. I went to a dance once in junior high and felt like I was alone in this room full of people. No one wants to be seen with me."

I have been in that room, a room full of people but all alone. I begged for the room to split open and swallow me.

The following day Harper handed me a small photo book.

I studied each photo after school that day. Harper shoved cake in her mouth on her first birthday. Then she ate a turkey leg larger than her leg at her first Thanksgiving. In a photo of her around fifth grade, her dim eyes shone with a smile, but something distracted her from the party. The remaining photos portrayed no variations except for age. One candid photo pictured her finishing off the pizza and eating leftover cake and ice cream. I saw melancholy in these cameos of her growing years and heard a cry of desperation.

The next day Harper and I discussed the photos.

"My pictures are all with food," she said. "Sometimes I can't even taste it. I think I'll try a new diet I read about. I can do it this summer. It seems easier than some other ones I've tried."

"Do your parents know how you feel?"

"Yes, Mom helps the best she can. I just find food, but she knows that too."

"Have you seen a doctor about your eating?"

"Yep."

"Did she do blood work?" I asked.

Harper's speech was soft and unexpressive. "Yep. Everything is normal. There's nothing wrong with me. Like it's in my head. Food's my comfort and hugs. Mom and Dad tell me to just quit. They don't get it. I can't. I considered quitting my job and dropping out of school. But you'd probably chase me down. I'm so embarrassed by how I look."

"Correct. I would pester you and your parents. Have you considered another doctor?"

"No. I gotta get to work."

Summer came and went and so did her diet.

Harper's senior year was one with an influx of eating changes. Nothing worked. It was in April that Harper and I had our last lunch together.

"I look in the mirror with disappointment. I am fat and ugly," she said, her voice quivering as tears rolled down her cheeks.

"Lasting beauty is not what you look like. It is in your character, deep in your heart," I mustered.

⟨⟩

Three years after Harper graduated, she knocked on my door.

"Harper, what a surprise. Please come in," I said, hugging her.

"Daily I struggled. Daily I failed," she began. "I was at a low point, sobbing and crying. I was ugly and doubted myself at every turn. Then I remembered your words—another doctor, lab tests. I have a rare disorder that caused my food cravings and weight gain. The doctor put me on medicine that helps control it."

Harper was scheduled for bariatric surgery the next week. I smiled and squeezed her hand.

"You listened to me even when I didn't talk," she continued. "But, most of all, I remember the last few words you spoke to me: 'Lasting beauty is not what you look like. It's in your character, deep in your heart.' "

"I didn't think you listened," I said.

"I listened to everything you said."

Eighteen months later, I received an invitation to her college graduation. The beautiful printed words were done over a light-shaded butterfly watermark. Its wings were spread in flight, delicate as silk paper.

VOICES

Zoey was a rather fragile student who radiated despondency through her porcelain skin and heavy brown eyes. She reminded me of a swan's feather, so slight and weak that a breeze might blow her away. She seemed overwhelmed with fear, trying to keep secret her suffering and torment. The one joy she appeared to have was assisting her struggling classmates with lab skills.

I was pleased when she wanted to talk one afternoon. With a guarded smile Zoey shared her dream to be a pediatric nurse, her dream to leave home.

"I was first raped when I was eleven years old, and I am still being raped. At first I didn't even know what was happening, just that I didn't like it and that it hurt. My mom won't believe me. She gets mad when I tell her about it. And sometimes she even screams at my brother, Todd, for no reason. I think she's tired from working so much, but Todd thinks she's just mean."

Zoey cried because of what had been stolen from her, and I feared what she was missing or may miss in life: inner peace, joy, a devoted love, success.

Those who knew Zoey's secrets were few: only her mother, the perpetrator, and me. I asked about Child Protective Services.

"Oh, they visit, but we all tell them everything is fine. We make it all look good and smile. Mom says we have to and I can't hurt her. She's had a hard life. If she loses this job she and I will have nowhere to live. You see, we live with this family: Valerie and her daughter, Susan. Been there six years now. My older brother's not there much. Mom's the housekeeper and I do other things to help out." She sat across from me, eyes downcast. "I know I shouldn't struggle so much with this. It's probably so insignificant compared to others' problems."

"Zoey, it is not insignificant," I assured her. "You've been traumatized and abused. I'm glad you were able to share it with me," I said, placing my hand over hers, the only comfort I knew to offer.

Zoey had no ride home, so I phoned my family to let them know I would be late.

We left the freeway for the narrow back roads and the rolling ominous clouds warned me of what was yet to come.

Rain drenched the ground and cold, merciless winds whipped from the west. The countryside rolled and dipped, curved and climbed. I skirted fallen tree limbs and swerved around narrow channels vomiting bubbles of muddy water. I gripped the steering wheel and Zoey clutched her seat. I wanted to be in the safety and warmth of home. But I was here, wherever here was.

"Well…you'll meet my mom, Erin," Zoey said. "She works for George and Valerie who own the home we live in. They've been good to us, ya know. Mom does all the household chores and manages their financial affairs. Things fell apart for us when Mom lost her job at the plant. She was the company's financial manager. Then Dad got sick and I guess the medical bills were a lot. Now we get fed and Mom gets paid. I love my mom, ya know. Anyway, George is a really important man. When he speaks people listen. I know we do." Zoey's tone changed from tender to melancholy. "He likes me to do his exercises for him. He's got an old war injury, ya know."

"And is that okay with you?" I asked.

"Well, I guess so. Mom and I have to live somewhere. George and Valerie's daughter, Susan, say it's just better to do what he says when he says it. My brother, Todd, doesn't stay there much. He just up and left one night. Said he'll make it on his own."

"I see."

We drove for an hour and I thought about how far Zoey rode the school bus every day, the amount of misused time. Then I spotted her house with the porch light on.

Erin greeted me at the weather-beaten door. Her wiry hair was tones of gray mixed with strands of brown. She wore a yellow sweatshirt that blended with her oatmeal skin and baggy sweatpants to hide her small, thin frame. Throw rugs were scattered about the worn wooden floors and there were cracks in the plaster and paint peeling from the walls, but everything was clean and neat. It was a lovely, humble home.

Something black sprinted past the doorway, then galloped the other way. I froze, pretending not to be afraid, and peeked around the corner.

"That's Thunder, a Great Dane," Erin told me.

He was well-formed, elegant, and regal.

"He is friendly," Zoey said.

Susan took Thunder and led me to the living area for cordial chit-chat. Thunder planted his head on her lap. Susan was in her early thirties and was short and stocky with cropped blond hair.

"I work here at home as a dog breeder," she said. "I've been out back with them. So far this year work has been slow. I want to work at a veterinarian's office and get my own apartment, but Dad likes me close to home. He's a Vietnam veteran and was elected a county commissioner last year."

"That's great. Where is your father, Susan?" I asked.

"He is in the back room getting ready for his exercises," she said.

Zoey stared at the door that never opens and didn't join the conversation.

Valerie, a small, ordinary woman whose dress sagged on her thin body, entered carrying a refreshment tray in her dry, cracked hands.

I smiled and took a sandwich though I found myself out of sorts and not hungry. We continued small talk about the weather, the dogs, Zoey's school work, and her twenty-two-year-old brother, who was not present. Valerie also kept watch on the door that never opens.

"I can see a bright future for Zoey," I said.

Her mother beamed with pride.

"The counselor will help her research resources to assist with college. There are also work-study programs. And I'll do some research too," I said.

The door that never opens, opened. George was present with his muscular six-foot-plus stance, rugged with a veneer of country lure. His shifty eyes displayed high, thick brows and a sinister sensation lingered about the room.

I approached him, extending my arm for a handshake as I introduced myself.

"I know who you are," he said. "Zoey will attend college if I say so and I'll pay for it."

His unwelcoming tone concerned me. "Sir, Zoey is intelligent and can have a successful life. It's very kind of you to pay, and she will qualify for some assistance also. She has dreams and goals to head toward," I said.

His eyes pierced my soul. My mind raced. My skin crawled. What is this aura of peculiarity? I still wasn't sure I understood the arrangement, their barter system.

His glare penetrated me.

"When I say something, no one is to question me. Do you understand?" he asked.

"No sir, I do not."

As he took a step toward me, he said, "Well, then maybe I need to teach you some respect."

"No sir, you do not. I respect you as a human being and a veteran. But I, too, deserve respect."

The room grew more tense with each round of words.

"You're a female who works. You need to be at home taking care of your man," he spat.

"Sir, women offer much to the workforce. And I have a wonderful husband who has no problem with me working. My father is the one who encouraged me to be educated. You might want to update some of your thinking."

"Like hell I will."

"Then it will be Susan and Zoey you keep behind closed doors. I feel badly for them regarding their future. I believe I have overstayed my welcome and must be leaving."

Two hours after my arrival, the storm persisted and I left more cynical and suspicious than I had arrived. I slipped Zoey my home phone number and told her to call anytime.

———

It was three in the morning. Zoey's words pulsed through every nerve of my body. I must keep her on the phone.

"...raped...again."

Those were the only words I understood through the weeping. I had to respond.

"Where are you now?"

"In my room."

"Close the door and lock it."

"It's closed but there's no way to lock it."

Of course not, I thought.

"Well, let's just talk then, Zoey. Does your brother happen to be there?"

"No, he visited earlier though." Her weeping grew louder and became deafening. "I can't do this anymore. I see no reason to live."

"Is your mother home to talk to you?"

"I guess. I don't need her with me. I can do this alone. Will you remember me?"

"Oh Zoey!" I cried. "No, you will not do this. Listen to me. Promise me you will come to school to see me. It's only about two more hours. Please, Zoey, answer me."

We both hung up sobbing.

Zoey exited the school bus in disarray, peering through wet puffy eyes and tugging at her crumpled T-shirt. We reported the abuse in the supervisor's office, but Child Protective Services could do nothing since Zoey had aged out of the system two months ago. So the supervisor phoned the police department and I excused myself.

"Do not give your phone number to students," the supervisor said. "And do not involve yourself in your students' lives. You are to teach and that's all."

"How can I educate when the students are unable to focus on anything but their own lives?" I fired back.

When questioned by the police, the family refuted the claim, made excuses, and provided alibis. And Zoey was too weak to defend herself so no charges were filed.

An undesirable outcome for Zoey seemed inevitable. I suggested she contact the suicide hotline but she wanted personal contact with someone she knew. I suggested a hostel or shelter, but she would not leave her mom.

Does no one hear her cry? Where are the voices for the voiceless? I wondered, overcome and broken down.

My colleague, Betty, suggested our two labs celebrate Thanksgiving with a feast.

The day of our celebration students arranged tables, placed handmade centerpieces, added place settings, and prepared side dishes. The turkey would soon arrive.

As we finished eating each student stood and named something he or she was thankful for.

When it was Zoey's turn she fixed her eyes on me and whispered, "I'm thankful for a teacher who listens to me, who is there when I need her. She is why I'm here today, why I live."

Her words roared in my head and the air became sour. What will happen to her? Who will listen, be her confidant? A precious life of innocence stolen.

As the fun-filled day came to a close, Zoey informed me that she was pregnant. Together, we sat in silence. There was nothing to say. Devastation has no limit. When would the death of destruction occur for young lives and for Zoey?

THE PROM GOWN

The morning's news report was a tragic scene of carnage.

"At approximately 10:30 p.m. on Saturday police officers were called to the scene of an accident on Potter's Mill Road. The crash occurred around 10:15 p.m. and involved two cars and a motorcycle. One person was killed, two were life-flighted to the nearest trauma center, and one was taken to the local hospital."

I only caught bits and pieces as the broadcast continued.

"An eastbound car veered left, rounding the bend...crashing... driver propelled through the windshield...pronounced dead by the coroner...injuring a passenger in oncoming car...driver and passenger airlifted...critical condition...oncoming cyclist...avoid the crash...lost control...thrown to the pavement...cause unclear...no names released."

My husband, Liam, listened to the interview with the 911 caller and told me that a package containing a beautiful prom gown was found on the scene.

Julie Wilmot had been voted prom queen but was flown to the trauma center and spent her senior prom night wearing a hospital gown accented by an IV and ventilator.

Four months later I was excited to greet September, the season when my senses prickle with the smell of apples and pumpkins and I listen for the rustle of fallen leaves.

But in September I faced the sting of melancholy when my supervisor, Mrs. Byron, announced that Julie would be in my class again that year.

"Her occupational therapist, her father, your health care instructor partner, Betty, and I feel this would be the easiest way for her to return to school since the accident," Mrs. Byron said. "According to her dad, Julie talked about you and your class all the time. She was excited to become a nurse. The doctors are not sure she'll fully recover from the traumatic brain injury (TBI) she sustained, but we all feel you can help with her recovery."

I wanted to object and couldn't believe that my friend, colleague, and partner in this educational mission, Betty, had forgotten to warn me.

I contacted Julie's occupational therapist, Peter McNally, and explained that I had only worked with TBI patients at life-threatening levels, but he had no reaction to my lack of experience besides saying he would send me information on educational rehabilitation.

The school year began in four days. I spent the evening on my computer researching TBI. A mass of notes peppered my desk, and books on various specialties covered the floor. I read until I couldn't any longer. I needed to speak with Julie's father before school began.

Mr. Wilmot combed through his personal horror to face the remnants of tragedy. The initial shock was now reality as he and Julie muddled along, bonding with the courage and resilience that came to matter most. Julie's younger brother and sister missed their mother and cried themselves to sleep, clinging to their father, unaware of the depth of his loss.

My lab doorknob clicked and Mr. Wilmot, wearing a navy blue suit and white shirt with a striking green pinstriped tie, entered with Julie just behind him. She stood tall but her eyes lacked luster and focus and her left leg swung out in an unsteady gait. She greeted me with a nod, a smile, and a big bear hug.

I had not seen her since the day she and her mother had gone prom gown shopping—the day of the accident.

Betty soon arrived and we all worked to develop an educational plan with attainable goals for Julie.

Mr. Wilmot said very little until he stood to leave, when he grabbed my hands and held them close to his chest, whispering, "Please, help Julie. She's not the same girl," as streams of tears flowed over his face.

"I'll do as much as I possibly can for her," I promised.

⊱✦⊰

Julie's speech was monotone, slow, and deliberate. A young girl once full of life now survived in apathy without dreams, but we set personal goals, her main one being to graduate from high school that year.

It quickly became apparent, though, that Julie was unable to follow more than one simple direction at a time. Alphabetizing files, following step-by-step handwashing or gloving instructions, and reading a one-line memo were unattainable. She was unable to move a wheelchair safely or lift a patient into bed. Although eye contact was poor and she bore no smile, there was a pleasantness to her demeanor.

I watched Julie drift down the hallway, invisible to those around her. Julie conversed with me regarding trivial subjects like the weather, her ride to school, and her clothing selections. But she preferred to be left alone, tuning out her new classmates and other sounds.

None of that would earn her a spot in health care. After four months of constant repetition, Julie's plan changed as my attempts for her success had failed. Mr. McNally tried another approach—on the job training.

As she left my lab I said, "You've had a big detour in life, Julie. But look at what you have and what you can do. Realize you can control that. Love has not ended and hope is not lost. Hope will never grieve you."

Julie visited from time to time and told me about her latest job placement.

Mr. McNally didn't stop until he'd found her a job where she could thrive. Julie landed at the hospital in cafeteria custodial work—wiping tables before, during, and after eating hours, then mopping the floor at the end of the day—and continued to work there for years, happy and smiling.

CUTTING TOOLS

At 7:30 a.m. I heard the faint sound of Leanne's mellow voice floating through the school atrium. She was practicing the national anthem alongside others who would be singing, speaking, and acting in the regional SkillsUSA meeting our school would soon host.

Later that morning I heard screams, shrieks, and profanity. My classroom door opened and in ran Leanne, whose voice was now harsh and gravelly, followed by Dayna, a masonry student. The girls rushed to my office to continue their argument, and I followed.

Leanne yelled, "Well, I'm the one they chose to sing the anthem, not you."

"You sound like a frog. Do you even know the tune? If I were you, I'd never sing in public. You're always off key," Dayna screamed back.

I'd heard enough and was losing patience and Leanne was crying. "Stop this!" I exclaimed sharply. "There is no excuse for your behavior. Who do you think you are? And what gives you any right to criticize Leanne?"

"I wouldn't even sing in the shower if I sang like you," Dayna continued.

I bellowed like a stampede of bulls racing across a field, "And you think you sound better? I should think not."

The second I spoke, I wished I could've stuffed those words back into my mouth.

Dayna ran from the room in tears, slamming the door, and Leanne continued to moan and weep.

After the students had left for the day, I reflected on how reckless, shortsighted, and out of line I had been. Was this the attitude I wanted to teach my students? I encourage positive character traits in students and create a classroom family, I thought. I had flattered myself, believing that my heart of intents was near perfect. This experience had shattered my ideals and I had traumatized Leanne and Dayna far more than they had traumatized each other.

The next day I found Dayna in the masonry lab and apologized.

Later I apologized to my class as well. "My hopes for this lab, for you as individuals, are not simple. But this disease of mistrust, the one I created yesterday through lack of self-control, will hang suspended in this room until kindness returns. There is a vast difference between an orderly classroom and an ostracizing one. I ask that you all consider this." I paused. "Now, get out your workbooks. Today's skill is on page ninety-seven."

⟞⟨⟩⟵

Leanne's words rolled over and over in my thoughts.

"I am not mean all the time. I just feel a big hole inside myself. Then I get mad and cry. I really want to become a famous and great singer but I can't. We're not rich and my family wants me in business. I see myself on stage and practice all the time when no one is home. I used to play piano and sing, but I don't play anymore.

I'm gonna sing in my church choir. I'll get to do solos. I'm sorry for wasting your time. I never told this to anyone. Please don't tell."

⊶⊷

Two days later Dayna resurfaced in my lab and asked if she could speak with Leanne.

"Of course," I said.

"Leanne, I am so sorry for the awful stuff I said to you. You really do sing well. I think you hit those high notes better than I would. I want to be a recording star, like for gospel music. I sing in our church choir now."

"I sing at church too. And someday I'm going to record songs too. Ya know, I think we should find another song for you to sing," Leanne said.

Then they both turned to me. "Wait a minute here. I'm not in charge of the regional meeting and there's only so much time allotted," I said.

They seemed disappointed but I had an idea.

Dayna missed the bus that afternoon and waited in my lab for her brother to taxi her home.

"Dad's a mason and has his own business," she said. "He wants me to work with him and learn the business. He won't listen to me sing. He keeps saying I'm not good enough. I think he's afraid I'll be a punk rocker. Anyway, he won't pay for me to have lessons."

So I asked Dayna to sing for me. Her smooth, powerful, mature voice rose to the ceiling, but she stopped mid-stanza, checked the clock, and left.

Before leaving that evening I approached Mr. Carney and shared the dilemma.

"Let them sing a duet," he said, "but only with approval from the superintendent."

Superintendent Mackey was, of course, hesitant.

"We've chosen Leanne to sing and the programs are printed," he argued.

"Yes, but Leanne would like for Dayna to sing with her. My lab can make a quick insert with the change for our program. Really, I think it would work."

"It's a hassle and you know it," he retorted. "Do you ever take no for an answer?"

"No sir, not when I'm advocating for students," I said, pleased at his concession.

I shared the good news with the girls the next day and they practiced together after school.

⋙⊹⋘

SkillsUSA regionals were held two days later and students competed to advance to the state competition.

Just before they took the stage, I wished Dayna and Leanne well.

Leanne spoke softly. "Our surprise is ready for everyone."

It was Dayna's first appearance outside of her church, and I told no one about the hassle to make the duet happen or the fuss to have Dayna's dad judge the brick-laying competition. That was perhaps the only way to get her parents and brother into the audience.

Leanne's and Dayna's voices rang out through the rafters. And then Leanne, after the first few lines, stepped back, giving the stage to Dayna—a surprise Leanne had devised on her own. Dayna was in the spotlight of an unknown beginning.

The competition ended and those in attendance filtered out after awards were presented. I overheard Dayna's father say, "I'm spellbound at the sound of your voice, Dayna. It's beautiful. I never really listened to you sing before. I am so sorry. Just know how proud I am of you. Shall we go celebrate?"

Dayna was acknowledged by her father and Leanne went home knowing she had helped her new friend.

Dayna's older brother, Josh, pulled into the slow stream of traffic and the car veered out of sight. I walked to my classroom aware that I play such a fleeting part in their lives, a small part to cut down or build up.

⋙⊹⊹⋘

Three weeks later the school received a letter asking for Leanne and Dayna to sing at the state competition.

THE POTTER'S KEY

Every ounce of self-worth clung to his chest, crushed by his monster.

After school, wide-eyed, unkempt Kyle entered my office and began speed talking.

"The voices intrude my thoughts. They're desperate and critical, mean and hurtful. I work hard to ignore them and figure out what is real and what isn't." He twirled his hand as if to shoo away an unwanted beast.

He sleepwalked to a place where nightmares replaced dreams and passed out in the dark under the stifling blanket of life.

"At night, it is my monster. In the day, it is my monster," Kyle continued. "I can't separate the nightmares from reality. The drugs started out feeling good with slow swirls of yellow, red, blue, pink, and green. Reaching a high was too much stimulation."

There was numbness at the summit, but in the valley it's a stumble into the fog.

Through his unraveling of family, loss of friends and relationships, and detachments from reality, I heard his voice of urgency over and over again.

Kyle left school five months later, in February of his junior year.

✥

The property was wired with cameras and security lighting. I made my routine visit to a specific room in the familiar building. The room smelled of fresh gray paint—intoxicating and clean—a smell that lingers only a few days. The closet doors had been rehung and painted black. His bookcase, opposite the bed and nightstand, was stacked with paperbacks, books on nursing, and his Bible. An old photo of his girlfriend, wrinkled from tears and Kyle's grip, lay on top of the bookcase. A new black door hung at the room's entry. The key, issued only to Kyle, hung at the nurses' desk with other residents' keys.

Four days earlier Kyle had ripped the gentlemen-riding-horses wallpaper from the walls, claiming that the horses were chasing him. He had also removed the closet doors and jumped on them like they were a trampoline, yelled obscenities at the doctor, and thrown a book at the counselor. He then kicked the wastebasket into the window, shattering it from corner to corner, and booted the cadet-green door to his room over and over. The outrage ended with him hurling toothpaste, cologne, hair gel, and coffee at the walls as he crumbled and collapsed in a corner and shook.

I remembered the words Kyle had scrawled on his school notebook late one Friday evening: "Why live? This is about nothing…quit telling me what to do…no one would miss me…I don't like this… pay attention…baby cries…sleepy…help…help me. KILL ME."

In this room—his room—we talked for hours about his life and the voices that controlled him, the destitution and wandering streets, the escapes and suicide attempts. His mind unraveled reality and placed him under siege with no direction, only inconsolable voices. A similar conversation ensued with each visit.

"I just don't think I can beat this thing," he said. "My mom and dad died a year or so ago, I think. Grandma and Grandpa threw me out years ago and I think they're dead too. Of course, they really weren't in my life anyway. I don't think they liked me very much. My girlfriend's gone. The government took the baby and I have no idea where he is. I have no job. I have no one. Couldn't even graduate from high school."

I nodded, unsure of what to say.

"I remember hiding in my closet, holding my hands over my ears, and squeezing my eyes shut to stop the images that came for me and told me what to do. I pulled the blankets over my head, hoping I could not be found before I suffocated."

"Oh, Kyle," I sympathized.

"I started to use drugs when I was eleven—weed and cocaine, even meth. I got it from my parents. Then by fifteen, I got my girlfriend pregnant. We did drugs together. She got hers from her parents."

I looked out the window and saw rain. "Kyle, I don't know what to say."

"After the baby, things just got worse. Just too much responsibility and no help. I was in a nightmare of bizarre images and terrible things. And the terror was I never woke up. The doctors here tell me it's psychotic. My thoughts were so jumbled. I tried to sort them out myself but couldn't."

⟢⟡⟣

I recalled another day in class.

"Something holds the wall up and those pictures help," he had said. "The walls are going to collapse and crush us."

His anxiety had piqued. He mumbled to himself, covered his head with his arms, collapsed to the floor, and crawled under his chair while talking in odd, incomprehensible speech.

⇥⇤

"I left school one day and drove for days without telling anyone where I was. No one looked for me except you. Then the cops found me on some back road in Kansas in my car. The car told me to just drive, so I did. I thought I didn't need food or sleep, but I was starving and exhausted after four days. I wanted to die. After that I knew I was no good and that nobody gave a crap about me. I gave up on life. I was so afraid. Still am."

He shifted his gaze to a blank wall, as if wishing to be absorbed into his marginal world. It was then I noticed how thin he had become. The jeans and T-shirt he wore gave him a well-groomed appearance, though his chestnut eyes appeared opaque and his skin looked like frosted glass.

Kyle twirled his curly hair at the nape of his neck, and, time and time again, he stood and walked to the door intently.

In a soft tone, I called his name.

He muttered words that sounded like "Stay away from me" and twirled his hand to shoo something away before he turned to me rather abruptly, leaving his collision of voices.

"I take lots of drugs now," he said. "The doc gives them to me even though I feel them in my feet and crawling up to my head. I want to explode. I can't. I can barely move or think, and I don't care about anything or anybody. I'm sometimes not sure who or where I am. I really need a cigarette."

"I cannot help you with that, Kyle," I said.

"If I could just get off this medicine, I could show them I'm not sick. I've tried before but they always catch me. They have cameras everywhere. You saw them. Someone is always watching me."

"Does that make you anxious?" I asked.

"What do you think? How would you like it?"

"Kyle, I can't relate to what you're telling me, but isn't life unclear and more confusing for you without your meds?"

He did not answer.

"Let's go down the hall," he said. "I want to show you what I'm doing now." He picked up his Bible and we left the room. "People here get religion. I did. Every day is a miracle I'm alive. It's just that...well...I'm not really worthy of living. I'm just no good."

We travelled long intersecting corridors that passed and crossed each other—an intricate maze of bewilderment, a jumbled web. We passed residents' rooms, the kitchen, two eating areas, a visitors' lounge, and a door to the private grounds. I glanced at the residents we passed. No one looked up or was aware of anyone else. No one spoke. We might never have been there.

We stopped at a locked door and Kyle proudly showed me his skeleton key to the art room. We stepped into a spacious, airy room with high ceilings and floor-to-ceiling windows—a view of the gardens, edged with arbor vitae and maples. Peonies, hostas, and irises dotted the area among stretches of shrubs, and geraniums in colorful urns were interspersed among ornate water fountains. Central to the garden was a gazebo. All of this was new for Kyle.

He led me to the potter's wheel, where a rugged yet fragile, substantial but wispy work was in progress.

He sculpted reality out of clay, a reality that reflected his thoughts, perhaps the way his world works? I recalled Isaiah 64:8. "We are the clay, you are the potter; we are all the work of your hand."

Kyle began to knead a mass of clay. Then he attached a metal plate to the wheel, placed the clay in the center, and added a bit of water. He made a hole in it as the wheel spun until a small odd-shaped pot was formed. After the pot dried Kyle chiseled away the excess clay. Features that do not belong break down, weakening the vessel until it collapses.

Time melted away as Kyle explained the firing process and then pulled a finished pot, complete with his signature and the date, from his work area for me, a gift of Kyle's existence, a reminder of his reality, a reminder of hope.

SILHOUETTES

The day began clear, colorful, and crisp with mist glistening on the fields. Toothless pumpkins perched on desks and students dressed in creative costumes fostered a festive tone.

Missy donned a red yarn wig and worn blue floral tablecloth covered by a stained chef's apron. She smiled with ruby red lips, freckles sitting atop her pink cheeks.

"I'm Raggedy Ann," she giggled. "I always wanted a Raggedy Ann doll."

The three-to-five-year-olds from the school's childcare program paraded in costume through labs, and my students knew their responsibilities: talk with the children, let them listen to their heart with the stethoscope, weigh them, and measure their height.

After the morning's celebration Missy splayed herself on the restroom floor. Tears flowed, her chest heaved, and her cheeks blotched. Missy clutched me, waiting for relief and courage to meet the struggles ahead.

Through her sniffles I heard, "There's no money. I can't go to competition."

I recalled how Missy's spirit had been lifted when she earned a place on our school's SkillsUSA knowledge bowl team. The team had become a highlight in Missy's life, a place where she was accepted and succeeded, and I refused to accept that her hours of study and team commitment had all been for nothing.

Several months back, her classmates had approached me and wanted to help her study during class, and I gave in. Compassion for Missy stirred all our hearts.

That was the day several students alerted me of Missy's plight.

"Missy has three younger brothers and three younger sisters," Helen began. "Her dad died four years ago and her mom works night shift as a waitress at a local diner. Some of us give her clothes to wear. Our church helps them with clothes, too, and with other stuff. They're always moving from place to place. Sometimes Missy tells us about how she has to take care of her brothers and sisters. She does all the cleaning and cooking, washes all their clothes, and makes sure they do homework and go to school."

Our impulse was to rescue her but there were no medications to give, no treatments to complete, and no poverty hotlines to call.

Emotions run high among teenagers but coping skills are in short supply. Add the underlying forces of inscrutable issues, and all I could do was quiet fears.

Over lunch I spilled my thoughts to Miss Hailey, the special needs instructor.

"Missy's Individual Education Plan (IEP) is sparse and no parent has ever attended the yearly meetings," Miss Hailey said. "Her reading and math levels are elementary, but I do believe she is capable of learning with extra help. Shc has learned the information for the skills competition well, better than some other members in fact." Her dental care is nil. And her family doesn't meet

Medicaid requirements, so her medical care is nonexistent. Child Protective Services is aware, but there is nothing they can do."

There was no neglect, no money, and no support. I expected more—more from parents, schools, churches, volunteers, and the system.

⇥⇤

The day after Missy informed me of her financial problem, she told her classmates and her team that she was unable to attend competition.

My students refused to let that happen and made fundraising flyers to hand out to administration, faculty, staff, and students. And Carson convinced Mrs. James, the office secretary, to let him make an announcement over the PA system.

An abundance of dimes entered our treasury, and I was proud of my students' compassion and leadership, but we needed $375.

When my class suggested a garage sale, I balked: too much time and effort. But they stood firm and this was not the time to teach decision-making. So I sought permission from administration.

Two weeks later piles of boxes and bags of clutter gathered in the back corner of our lab, and the faint odor of local thrift shop fragranced the room.

Then one day a haggard slouching figure rummaged through our bits and pieces, inspecting each one and holding on to certain items. I cautiously inched to the back of the room and introduced myself to Ronnie, Missy's boyfriend.

"I'm searching for items for our home, mine and Missy's. We're gonna get married when I move out of my car. Get a place," he said, parading me outside to see his clunker—his pride and joy and sole possession.

A distinct odor wafted out as he opened the rusty driver's door, and a cloud cast a shadow over the day.

"I'm saving money so Missy and I can have a house—a real house—when we get married."

I smiled.

He wanted some of our gathered bits and pieces, so I gave Ronnie his choice items and said, "Consider these early wedding gifts from Missy's classmates."

He donned a wide smile and threw his arms around my waist and then gathered a lamp, a mixer, a comforter, and dishware. He rearranged his personal possessions, shoving the gifts around and between, and clunked down the lane.

⚊⚌⚊

Twenty-six-year-old Ronnie and Missy married six days ago, on Missy's eighteenth birthday.

"Ronnie has a number of health issues: a mitral valve replacement, a hernia, and hearing loss from being beaten as a child," Missy told me. "He tries to work, but he was fired as a paper deliverer when his car would not run. He missed three days so they got somebody else. He tells me it is all okay and things will get better."

Hearing loss was Ronnie's main problem, not the ill-fitting faded T-shirt with stains under each armpit that I struggled with. I could not let this man go nowhere in life.

I arranged for our auto-mechanic program students to repair his car at no cost and for our auto-body program students to paint the car. Then I phoned my connections to unearth a facility to help Ronnie. One was found, 180 miles away.

After school Ronnie phoned them from my lab. His appointment was three weeks later, the same week as our garage sale, and Helen loaned Ronnie her car for fear his couldn't make the trek.

The day of the garage sale finally arrived and we sold everything but a small bag of odds and ends. The students earned enough for Missy to attend the competition.

Two days after Ronnie's appointment, my supervisor asked, "What was that long-distance call you made?"

"A doctor for Ronnie," I said. I knew I was wrong. The phone was for school use only. "I am sorry. I guess I wasn't thinking. I'll pay the charge, just let me know what it is."

He left the room without comment.

＝≺ᛁ ᛁ≻＝

State competition day arrived. Missy was unable to eat and sleep and her breaths became shallow and rapid as she travelled a new road. She borrowed a suitcase, spent time away from home, and slept two nights in a hotel riding on her classmates' support. She saw our state capital and toured the capitol building. She was a team member, and she cheered for our school's competitors. Our school cheered for her and her team won a gold medal.

Missy's happy moment prevailed for two months until she started failing lab, which disqualified her from the senior lab the following year. I forced myself to talk with her.

"Missy, perhaps the food service program would be better? Or child care?"

She blurted out, "I'm pregnant. I don't want to be yet. I can't raise a baby this way."

Trying to guide her and give comfort and strength, my voice quivered, then lapsed to silent as we shed tears together, again.

The following year Missy entered the culinary program and delivered a healthy boy in December that they named Chad. And she was able to finish her senior year.

＝≺ᛁ ᛁ≻＝

Three years later Missy phoned and asked me to visit them for dinner. I drove down the unpaved one-lane side road through the trailer park at a snail's pace. It was an unsightly place, a place where the penniless and impoverished resided. The area was full of street-corner neighbors wearing baggy pants, chains, and ball caps placed sideways on their heads.

Ronnie's voice cried out from within their home inviting me in. I greeted him with a fruit basket, noting his disheveled appearance, and I saw Missy in jeans and a holey WWJD T-shirt playing with Chad.

We conversed over dinner—a hot dog and beans—as I noticed the sparseness of the house, the worn carpet, the lack of pictures, and an unfilled refrigerator and cupboards. Ronnie's hearing was improved. And he drove another clunker, this one five years newer. He and Missy both had jobs they liked. Missy was a dishwasher hoping to become a cook, and Ronnie bussed tables at the same diner.

"The owners give us leftovers three times a week. And we dig in the trash if we see something edible," explained Ronnie.

They struggled to provide food for Chad, make house payments, and drive to work. I sensed unmistakable tugs on my heartstrings.

Ronnie said, "We love each other and Chad. We're so happy. What more is there?"

Missy added, "And we go to church—Helen's church. It's good to have Chad grow up in a church. I don't want him in the same situations Ronnie and I were in. That's why I wear this T-shirt. It makes me ask myself, 'What would Jesus do?' "

I stood on the street and looked back at their home, shadows of poverty and wealth and struggle and success amid three silhouettes in the doorway. But, above all, I saw rays of love and joy and faith and peace.

I drove home and mobilized my family for a brisk neighborhood walk. We heard the pigs snort and slop about in their pen, and the cows walked the pasture without a worry, ignoring our presence. The wind blew maple seed pods around us in whirly-bird motion. We enjoyed simple pleasures and were thankful to be together. Cattails grew from a low-lying flooded edge of grass, and the moonlight cast them as silhouettes. They danced and waved, gracing the night with hope.

AWAKENING SECRETS

An hour after students had left for the day, Shea, a graphic arts student, stood at my office door interrupting my monotonous grading. Her spirited voice became strange noises and her left arm twitched as she gurgled and collapsed. Then her eyes rolled, her head thrashed side to side, her jaw stiffened, and her teeth clenched like a vice around wood.

I put my sweater under her head and yelled for help. Supervisor Jack phoned Shea's mother, Mrs. Mills, and she came to take Shea home.

Shea recovered and said, "Mom told my home school, all my teachers here at the career center, and my whole family that the seizures are not real. She thinks I make them up."

Words from my early days in nursing echoed in my head. "Always believe the patient. Observe the symptoms."

"Have you seen a doctor?" I asked.

"Nope."

Mrs. Mills, a small, sparrow-like, eagle-eyed woman, went straight to Shea and hugged her before they marched away hand in hand. I followed, describing Shea's seizure since her mother hadn't so much as acknowledged me. I told her about seizures, the possibility of untreated epilepsy with long-term effects, and suggested that Shea see a doctor.

Shea shrugged and raised her eyebrows in defeat when her mom became upset with me.

The next morning Supervisor Jack came to my office.

"Mrs. Mills doesn't want Shea taken to the hospital and you can't disrespect her choice," he said.

"I do respect her and her choice. But, sir, she is running from the truth and making excuses. Seizures can't be ignored. And what about Shea's choice?"

He left my office after twenty minutes, thinking I agreed. Still, doubt consumed my thoughts. What do I do if Shea has another seizure? I have a responsibility to protect students. Experience told me that not to take action was wrong.

As the year moved on, Shea experienced several more seizures. One was in the guidance office at school and I dialed 911. Shea squeezed my hand as the paramedics carried her out on a gurney and started her on oxygen. Mrs. Mills fumed and I was reprimanded again, this time in writing placed in my file.

Two days later Shea phoned me from the hospital.

"Doctor Smyth diagnosed me with epilepsy. He ordered medication for me but my mom doesn't want me to take it. She won't get it for me 'cause people will look at me funny. Like, I just want to be normal. And, well, my mom is really mad at you."

Administrative words from the past—words I had ignored—rang clear in my head. "Leave this alone. You cause problems when you interfere in the students' lives. And all you do is enable them. Sometimes it's better not to know or ask questions."

I arrived at the hospital and walked in silence to Shea's room.

"No visiting," Supervisor Jack had said. But how could I not?

Shea was alone and scooted to a more upright position when I entered.

"I'm takin' the meds now and I feel better," she said. "The doctors and nurses wanna watch me for a few more days."

"You look more rested than when I last saw you," I said.

"My mom is always at work. It's just us and I wish she had more time for me. I'm not sure she loves me enough to be with me."

"Shea, you need to tell your mom how you feel," I said, handing her the cards her classmates had sent.

As she looked through them, the door opened. Mrs. Mills stepped to her daughter's bedside scowling at me. She nodded toward the door and we stepped outside.

She lit up a cigarette and spoke between the puffs. "I tried to quit years ago. No reason to disapprove just because you're a nurse. I know I shouldn't."

I tasted her bitterness with each puff.

"I knew you'd come see her. My instinct was to have staff stop you at the door and escort you out. You've humiliated us and my family pities us now because of Shea's illness. Want to help Shea, do you?"

"Yes, I do."

"Well, we were fine until you interfered. We live in a small community and it's a struggle not to be normal. Shea is normal."

"I agree. Shea is normal. She has a medical condition that can be treated."

"I'm the chief financial officer here so now the whole building knows and everybody keeps asking questions. They're a bunch of busybodies. Shea's classmates will laugh at her. And it's your fault. I could've kept this a secret. Well, I'm embarrassed and ashamed. And Shea makes me a failure."

"The students do not laugh at Shea; they worry about her. She's very likeable. And her having epilepsy does not mean you are a failure. It's not your fault. Without treatment Shea will have difficulty holding a job. She won't be able to drive a car. It's not safe. But with proper treatment she can have a normal life."

In sorrow she looked at me and said, "Her seizures are so ugly to watch."

"A seizure is not a pretty sight. But with medication they can be controlled. And those sticky prejudices of the past are not what we see today. People are more educated. No one will judge you, and your years with Shea are slipping away."

I didn't know what more to say as I watched the sullen tears roll down her face.

When her eyes cleared, she said, "Leave. And don't return."

A month later Mrs. Mills called me.

"Thank you," she said, then hung up.

Shea remained on her medication and her seizures were under control. She stopped in my lab often to visit.

Two years later I bumped into Mrs. Mills at the hospital. She smiled and told me that Shea was doing well both physically and with her college courses.

PART THREE

a time to weep, and a time to laugh;
a time to mourn, and a time to dance...

Ecclesiastes 3:4 ESV

WOLVES

S *LAM.* The explosive force sliced through the morning chaos. Celeste darted into the locker room, her jellies slapping the floor in her rush.

"It's all I have, like I don't have anything else to wear. I'll fail, I'll fail," she screamed, sobbing.

The students encircled her in a teenage pack to reassure, console, and cheer her. A pair of eyes pierced my back, and I turned to see a wolf in disguise, Mrs. Fisher: science instructor, self-assigned hallway monitor, and dress code enforcer. The corners of her mouth turned down and her brow peaked in wrinkles.

Group panic set in as Wolf Fisher lunged forward, growling, "That girl is in dress code violation. I want to see her now. She needs to be sent home."

In bogus calm I said, "Her name is Celeste. And I can handle the situation."

Wolf Fisher snarled as my heart pounded and muscles tightened.

"I'll report this and Celeste will be in the office, along with you," she threatened.

SLAM. Another blow hit the air as Mrs. Fisher left. The students stood spellbound, Celeste defeated.

"I have to dress up today 'cause it's my day to give my speech in English class, and if I dress up I get more points," Celeste said. "Like, this is the only thing I have to wear and I need those points. Do I really look that bad? Like, am I fat? Mrs. Fisher said my skirt is too short and tight. I feel ugly."

A lone wolf had shredded its prey.

"Respect is not about what is easy, it is about what is essential," I said, beginning an impromptu character-building lesson. I reviewed respect for school rules regarding attire, respect for all teachers, and respect for each other. "It is how the classroom operates to guide young minds."

The once-timid class presented a plan. Celeste wriggled her skirt down over her hips as far as possible and Sue rummaged in her locker for a blouse for Celeste to wear. The blouse covered her hips and the upper part of the skirt. I sent Janice to locate an iron and we added my lab jacket for a more professional appearance. Karrie fixed Celeste's hair and applied a little makeup. Celeste met school dress code and looked beautiful in a haphazard sort of way, or so I thought.

⊱⊰

It was late that night when Celeste walked home from a friend's house after studying for their seventh grade history exam. They had spent extra time together playing with makeup and hair. But she knew the path by the donut shop and the Hennesseys' home.

She recalled the shadows across the street—more than one, three—as she recounted her trauma to me.

"When I regained consciousness, I was naked on my back on the sidewalk and couldn't move my arms or legs for someone holding me down."

I swallowed hard as Celeste struggled to go on. We sat in silence for a time, her hand in mine.

"The boy on the left tried to force me to have oral sex. So did the boy on the right. I turned away and clamped my mouth shut as tight as I could. But the third boy raped me."

More silence filled my office.

"I screamed for help and begged them to stop. Yet no one responded to my cry."

"Celeste, I really don't know what to say," I managed to utter.

Wiping away her tears, she said, "I'm just glad I finally told someone. I knew those boys. Two are in college now and the other one works around here in construction." She mumbled through tears, staring at the jellies on her feet. "It is awful. They're older now. I know them and don't see them, but this morning I ran into one of them. I am scared. I try not to think about it but I have flashbacks and nightmares and wake in sweat. I hear them laugh as they unzip their pants and I smell their stink. I babysit my two younger sisters after school. I'm afraid for them. Mom works at the bar all evening and night. We don't have much. I didn't report it. I won't, I can't."

Her hands gripped the arms of my office chair, her body trembling. Celeste became a target that night—a victim of gang rape—at age twelve.

⛗

Some teachers thought Celeste was aloof or rebellious with incomplete assignments and drifting from friends, but she was at war with herself. She wanted peace and needed love. She felt weak and helpless and had no support system outside of school.

Her mom did what little she could but school assistance, faith-based support, and public-funded therapies had waiting lists. Economics and fear barricaded Celeste's hope and healing.

Some teachers disciplined but detention and suspension were only rejection. Celeste's emotional trauma and humiliation continued to build and life became tiresome.

She began spending lunchtime in the haven of my office, where she searched for her dreams, joy, and optimism.

She said, "I would like to know who I am. And I want to know, why me?"

There was no escape from her torment. She lived in anguish from her scars.

"Celeste, do you feel any relief after telling me about your rape?" I asked.

"I wouldn't say that, but maybe I'm a tiny bit more confident," she answered. "But still, some days, I feel hopeless and think my life is just wasted."

"You really should talk to a counselor," I urged.

"I am afraid to graduate, but I do have a little scholarship money and I qualify for grants. I'm determined to succeed. You've given me that. No matter what I ever did in class or here at school, you supported me, gave me wisdom and knowledge, and, most of all, made me look at myself. That's not easy to do 'cause I don't like what I see."

Something about Celeste, perhaps the angle of her shoulders and the auburn curls that framed her soft smile, suggested she embodied a silent strength. Yet I wondered when her mind would resolve the self-judgment and guilt.

Celeste graduated with the goal of becoming a youth counselor. She had found hope.

MAGIC KEYS

Six-foot-two Zeke stood in my lab, his bright blue eyes flashing a cutthroat glare from his blotchy, craggy face. He commanded presence among his classmates, luring them in with the mysterious and enthralling them in whatever conversation he graced them with.

The basketball coach cut Zeke from the team for behavior and poor grades. In my lab he did no skills or written assignments but frequented the computer more than the assigned times permitted. He pouted when I asked him to work and threw his books at the nearest object or me. Curse words resided on the tip of his tongue and he pointed at me, making an evil, vengeful threat.

Administration removed Zeke and gave him a one-day detention.

⟞┼⟝

When Zeke returned to class, I caught him red-handed, absorbed in the pictures on the screen so intently that he never saw me approach. When I spoke, he hid the screen.

"It popped up by accident. I'd never look at stuff like this," he said.

I contacted the supervisor while Zeke brooded.

"Don't get so bent out of shape. Nothin' I ain't seen before," Zeke called out.

His sinister smile revealed glimpses of a corrupt young mind, and I wished there was a piece of technology to correct his behavior.

Zeke returned to school in five days, hardened and unreachable. I reminded him for six days to wear his uniform. Are rules unimportant to him?

The next Tuesday and each day after, he arrived in a messy, rumpled uniform. As the days passed, I detected bagginess in his pants and looseness in his shirt. His once docile hair became an unruly mane. His grades continued to drop, and any bit of composure Zeke held vanished as his actions escalated toward violence.

While eating lunch with his buddies, he jumped out of his seat, punched a friend in the face, and ran from the room. In the hallway Zeke collapsed in a seizure.

I waited for his mom to phone from the hospital.

"They found drugs in his blood," she reported with a tremor in her voice. "I don't understand. I can't lose him."

"It's not easy raising a son alone," I said, trying to comfort her.

When Zeke was fourteen, his father had gone to prison for assault, battery, domestic violence, and gunrunning.

"Zeke seems fragile, selfish, and captivated by his pleasures," I said. "Give him your love, support, and guidance."

The school rejected Zeke again with a one-week suspension. Has Zeke lost all moral values? Has he lost himself? I wondered.

Upon his return, I suggested that he transfer to another lab.

"I hate this lab and don't want to be here," he said. "I want to build things like my dad. He was a carpenter and showed me how to be one too. My mom wants me to be nothing like my dad, though, so she put me in this one."

I attempted a lab change to follow a student's dream, if that's what it was, but administration denied it. The dream was all Zeke had.

Days passed. He violated computer rules for the second time on another porn site. He was a frequent flier of such places.

Zeke sneered, laughed, made derogatory remarks about me to the class, and cursed at me. The students looked at him with saucer-sized eyes. Has he lost every ounce of respect for authority?

His life sped out of control with more unbalanced curves ahead. Another suspension—two weeks this time.

Zeke returned ten days later without his uniform. He was miserable in my lab. How do I deal with him?

Administration said, "Lay down the law."

His mom said, "You have to understand him."

And the guidance counselor said, "Maintain power, set boundaries, listen to him, focus on him, make him feel important and valuable, and let him solve his own problems."

I tried every idea, thought, and theory to no avail. Still, administration would not let him change labs.

Then I learned that Zeke was going to be a father. But he didn't care. He broke up with the girl. In the hallway they entangled in a slapping match, but then he laid her out cold.

I thought of the innocent baby as a hallway proctor hauled them to the office.

This time Zeke's mother sought a counselor for him, and I suggested she attend counseling as well. But she resisted.

Zeke was back in two weeks. And his girlfriend had returned a day earlier, sporting a yellowish-brown eye with a bit of puffiness about the side of her face. Most students avoided him.

I caught him again on a porn site, but he made no effort to hide his actions, as though to taunt me. Then he faced me and stepped closer, cursing me, the school, his classmates, and his mom. He dashed through the door and I contacted the supervisor.

Several hours later his mother arrived. She turned to the supervisor and pointed at me.

"It is her fault. She picks on Zeke. She doesn't want him in her lab. She doesn't like him," she exclaimed.

I tried to speak, but she continued her banter.

"We have a hard life without his dad. It's better that way. But I barely make enough money to live on. He should be given some space to do what he wants."

Zeke was expelled.

I stood in my world with my students thinking of the young man we had just lost, his shell and the fragileness within him shattered. I thought of the hours Zeke had spent on a computer, the days his dad had spent in prison, and the time the coach had spent with him. I thought of the hours I had spent with him and the years his mother had devoted to him. If there was to be blame, we all had it wrong.

⚊⚔⚊

It was quiet and my energy had returned. I cleaned the lab and went through my file cabinets, throwing out unnecessary paper. I scrubbed the storeroom, the hospital beds, and the desks and rearranged the linen and storage closets, lugging outdated materials to the closest garbage bin.

Kalen saw me and helped me give a final heave into the bin. As he walked away, I heard him say, "Key didn't work, huh?"

⚊⚔⚊

On Saturday's news the television anchor announced breaking news.

"A local boy lost his life Saturday morning at 2:57 a.m. on Highway 23A. His name has not been released. He was driving his mother's 1995 Dodge Ram. The pickup entered the turn at a high rate of speed, went airborne over a drainage ditch, and collided with a tree fifty feet away. The driver was not wearing a seat belt and there were no passengers. Alcohol and drugs are believed to have been factors. The road remains closed for further investigation."

More news continued but was interrupted with, "We have just learned that the young man in the car accident was eighteen-year-old Zeke..."

THE FOG

Tall and slender with black silky hair, Lori's olive complexion drew attention to her steel gray eyes.

Six days ago I'd noticed her withdrawal from others. Her classmates no longer gathered at her desk to review for a test, and Lori dawdled about the lab unable to complete assigned skills. She missed classwork while nodding off, so she needed to copy notes.

Our linen closet needed straightening, so I assigned Lori to the task. She pursed her lips and breathed deeply.

"I do not sleep well at night," she said to me, task half-done. "I'm often awake when the sun comes up."

When I asked why, she shrugged and left when class was over.

Lori was absent several days and finishing the linen closet waited.

When she returned she arrived twenty minutes early, her eyes open wide with dark circles underneath and her hair tangled like she'd just disembarked a roller coaster ride.

She chatted with classmates and tried to take over class discussions, but it was difficult to decipher her writing and her lab skills were sloppily done, as was the linen closet. It seemed a struggle for her to focus, like she existed in rapid moments of joy.

⊷⊶

It was time for our student panel discussion on euthanasia. Panelists took their places and presentations commenced. Lori stopped mid-question, looking to the left side of the room. No one was there and nothing appeared out of order but Lori stood, stomped, and argued with classmates over disagreeing opinions.

She pointed at them and faced left, screaming, "I don't really care what you believe. I don't care what any of you think," before storming out of the room.

I was certain the door broke when she slung it open, gouging the doorknob into the adjacent wall and chipping the paint. What extreme sensitivity and agitation. There was no problem present. It seemed created.

The next day I called Lori into my office.

"Lori, you seem to have had some not-so-good moments lately," I said.

"Yeah, I know. I stare at the wall all night, hoping to find some answers within myself," she replied. "At the first sign of daylight, I get out of bed feeling anxious or angry. On my way to school I tell myself to focus, pay more attention to my school work."

"And how does that work for you?"

"It doesn't. I just don't want anyone or anything controlling me."

"What is controlling you, Lori?" I inquired.

"My medication. I pretend to take it. Sometimes we don't have it. But when I do take it, I feel foggy."

"Why don't you have the medicine?"

"My parents can't always afford it, and, like I said, it puts me in a fog. I fought with my psychologist. Somedays I don't think I'm really here. I can't control myself an' nobody listens."

"How long have you been seeing a psychologist?"

"I can't remember. He said I'm bipolar," she admitted. "At first my parents didn't want to believe it. But I knew something was wrong and that's when I started taking medicine—when they could pay for it. I just want to be normal."

I informed my supervisor.

A week later Lori's mother, Mrs. Carothers, came for a conference. The curly brown hair that edged her face softened the wrinkles of her worry and black-framed glasses hid the dark circles of interrupted sleep.

"As a young child, Lori held my hand on the way to the park, squealing with delight," Mrs. Carothers began. "She loved having me push her on the swings. She smiled and giggled, pretending she was a bird and then we hugged and squeezed each other when she safely landed. As she went to seventh grade, she still talked with me about friends, boys, and school. And we took art classes together. But in her early teens, there were subtle changes. Lori became distant from me and displayed anger and rage toward her father. I thought it was just her hormones or a phase, but then she ate less and less and her sleep was interrupted. James and I figured she wasn't going to change without help."

Mrs. Carothers fought back tears when I explained that I would need to report the medication Lori was taking, and she asked that I discreetly inform only directly involved instructors.

"I've had people say Lori is just spoiled...on drugs...runs with the wrong crowd...has no future. It hurts," Mrs. Carothers said.

It pained me that my colleagues were not aware of Lori's history.

Several weeks later Mrs. Carothers phoned.

"James was laid off last week," she said before handing the phone to Lori's dad.

Mr. Carothers said, "For four years we've fought with Lori: arguments, hysterical reactions, refusal to be near us or go anywhere with us. She'd lock herself away except when she wanted to scream.

My wife and I stood firm, together. But in the past few weeks, Lori's quit takin' her medicine altogether and started believing in outer space people. Says they're in a plot with the school and government to take over the world. Controlling all farms is the first move. Next they'll control our communication satellites, then seize our electricity. We'll have no thoughts of our own. The doctor calls it delusional beliefs and paranoia."

I was speechless.

Mr. Carothers went on. "One night the police phoned us, and we rushed to the station. An officer had charged Lori with shoplifting. She cursed us and the police, saying we were all part of the plot. All her mom could do was cry. Two weeks later Lori locked her bedroom door and sneaked out a window."

Lori's parents wanted her to continue to take her medication and attend counseling, but their savings was gone. Mrs. Carothers income was from a part-time retail job.

Again I informed the supervisor.

Several weeks later I received an email from my supervisor. "Spoke with Lori's father. She's been absent with upper respiratory infection...is bipolar...psychologist moved and no new orders, but can't afford the medicine."

Where do we find help for Lori and her family?

His email continued. "Lori is paranoid and very sensitive and becomes agitated very easily—perceiving problems when none exist. Her sleep habits are interrupted each night."

I contacted our guidance counselor, and, within two weeks, she had found financial assistance for Lori's treatment. And the Carothers found a new psychologist.

We all devised a plan for Lori. When her emotions were escalating, I would phone the supervisor to escort her to the guidance office. And the psychologist began a new care plan and new medications. Lori was permitted to keep a water bottle at her desk and leave class at her discretion due to possible bouts of intestinal upset.

Some days her ability dulled yet I noticed the renewing of friendships. According to her mother Lori's appetite had improved and she even had a slight weight increase. Her sleep pattern had also improved but she still had moments of fatigue. Within a month, the psychiatrist believed her medication was well-regulated and he began seeing slow improvement.

I perceived hope while Lori grasped joy.

MISSED SIGNS

Packed among the equipment and luggage in the school van assigned to me were Marika and Skylar as we headed to Capital City. I drove slower than the two lead vans, each transporting six students, all of whom were competitors at the state SkillsUSA competition. I drove that route every year, but that year, there were construction cones and detour signs.

Follow County Route 545.

Five miles later more warnings materialized.

Bridge Out Ahead. Temporary Route.

My sense of direction twisted and turned for two hours, failing me as I missed and misread signs.

When we finally arrived, we ate dinner in the hotel restaurant and then the students headed to their rooms. But Skylar soon returned, eyes bloodshot and puffy.

"It's my stupid sister, Willow," she cried, her fingers fidgeting.

I nodded. Sisters squabble. "What has she done that upset you?"

No answer. Skylar ran to her room.

What did I miss? I wondered, following her.

She opened the door before I knocked.

"Dad came home drunk again two nights ago. He went to Willow's room. That's where he always goes. She's younger and won't fight him off. I heard her whimper and tell him no. But he gets what he wants. He called her a whore, a tramp, a promiscuous something or other. Then I heard him slapping her. By the time I got to the room, Willow was curled up on the floor and he was kicking her in the stomach. I jumped on his back and tried to scratch his face. He threw me down the steps. I couldn't move. Willow got up from the floor and crawled back in bed. He closed her door and I laid there sobbing. I could do nothing."

I nodded and wiped my eyes, but Skylar wasn't done.

"I just talked to Willow and I'm so mad at her for giving in. She's just weak. He made her that way. She has no choice. As soon as I graduate I'm out of there. I'll take Willow with me. Why do you think I came here to compete? It was just to get away from him."

I phoned administration the next morning. My supervisor did what had to be done for Willow. But Skylar was eighteen and would remain in the house with her dad.

For two days, presentations, speeches, and skill competitions consumed our students. I made sure they arrived in order and on time. I ironed shirts, cleaned mud from shoes, put makeup over tattoos, braided hair, and cheered for each. For two days I applauded success and comforted loss.

As we travelled home, Skylar leaned forward and whispered, "Can you pull over? Marika's bleeding."

Marika told me she was about two months pregnant.

"I've been bleeding the past week," she said. "My back hurt me this weekend 'cause I stood a lot. I've been bleeding a little ever since I knew I was pregnant. I don't really feel pregnant. Not sure, though, how I should feel. I'm bleeding more now and have some cramps. Am I gonna lose the baby? Do I have to tell my mom?"

"Well, there's a possibility," I said. "And yes, you will need to tell your mom. You'll need to see a physician."

I pulled off at the next exit and drove to the nearest restaurant, where Skylar and I helped her into the restroom. The bleeding increased. Brown. Clots.

An hour later the bleeding slowed and Skylar dug through Marika's suitcase for clean clothes, and I phoned Marika's mother.

The silence between us spoke mother to mother. Two hours later we arrived in the school parking lot. Marika's mom hovered by her car door, arms crossed over her chest with lips pursed and eyebrows lowered.

"What have you gone and done?" she scolded. "Who's the father, that boyfriend of yours? How will you support…"

Marika lowered her head to shed tears and I waited at a distance. Soon the anger ceased and her mom embraced her tightly. Marika returned the hug and rested her head on her mother's shoulder.

A mother's broken heart. A daughter's sobs of sorrow.

But Skylar would have no hugs, only a daughter's sobs of sorrow.

How many more signs would I miss?

WRAPPED IN THE MUSIC

Brodie threw her notebook at me and her books to the floor and cursed anyone or anything in sight. Two glass panels crashed to the floor, shattering, when she slammed the door behind her.

What took seconds seemed to drag on for minutes as students stood around in shock.

This was great fodder for our two drama queens: the fair-haired, brown-eyed lover of tragedy and the dark-haired, hazel-eyed lover of self.

"Back to your physical therapy work, all of you, and focus," I ordered, phoning the office to report Brodie's episode.

The supervisors searched for her but she was nowhere to be found and was absent the next day too.

I stopped at the local coffee shop Brodie's Uncle Art owned. It was the only current contact information I had for her, and she worked there part-time but was off duty that evening.

After introducing myself and asking for an update on Brodie, Uncle Art said, "Brodie has no family contact but me. My sister has disowned her and the rest of the family just can't trust her. I let her sleep here in the back room."

"I'm sorry to hear that, but I do understand. I, too, have a difficult time with Brodie in class. She's so angry most days. I've tried to talk with her, but she'll have none of that."

"Brodie's boyfriend and father of her two-year-old son was convicted of armed robbery, trafficking illegal substances, and assault and battery and sentenced to three-to-six years in prison just yesterday," he said. "Brodie's son, Damon, is being adopted today by her aunt. Brodie blunders along the way. Yesterday she tried to escape Child Protective Services, and she got a couple states away. It's that kind of stuff that she's on parole for to begin with and why she wears that ankle bracelet. She's always trying to kidnap Damon, but he hasn't lived with her since he was born."

My forehead wrinkled and I bit my lower lip. "She never told me why she wore the ankle bracelet. Said she was set up by the cops."

Uncle Art said, "No one set her up. It's her own behavior. Anyway, we all thought that with an aunt as adoptive mother at least Brodie could be part of his life if she behaves."

⊨╬╠⊨

After threats of never seeing Damon, Brodie conceded and returned to school. She was excited about Christmas and looked forward to time with her son, even under the supervision of her aunt.

That Christmas season the welding lab had raised money for Toys for Tots. The fundraiser was a school dance, which Betty had convinced me to attend and Brodie had highly anticipated.

"I like to dance. I can cut loose like I'm all wrapped up in the music. I can breathe and I'm as happy as I can ever be," Brodie once told me.

I believed her, but she wouldn't be doing that at the fundraiser because no one knew where she was, again.

The students tried to teach Betty and me the latest moves, the Macarena.

My limbs were rusty and I lacked rhythm. I turned right when I should have turned left. I slapped one student and stomped on another's foot and then stepped on my own foot. I stumbled and splatted a belly smacker onto the gym floor. The crowd gathered and I heard giggles and loud laughter while captive to my shame. I never asked them to toss me overboard like this, these overzealous students. Brodie would have enjoyed my moment of humiliation, my impersonation of one who could dance.

━◁┼▷━

Two weeks later Brodie returned to lab, solemn and quiet. She refused to talk with our guidance counselor and barely acknowledged my presence. Her ankle bracelet was gone, but I sensed anger brewing.

Three days later she was absent again. In another week Brodie returned with another ankle bracelet. She had been caught using and selling illegal drugs. Her despondency festered, and she defied me at every turn. Brodie refused to help herself.

"Please, Brodie, put your shoes on in the lab," I asked. "You know our uniform policy."

"You're not fair. Life ain't fair. Everybody is against me. I get blamed for everythin' that goes wrong. School's a crappy waste. My fiancé's always wronged too. That's why he's in that dungeon of a screwed-up prison. But he's gonna break out and we're gettin' outa this dump," she fired back from her pity party. That drew in the drama queens. "Don't you dare tell me what to do an' don't try to stop me. You hate me. Well, I hate you too."

She ran from the room barefooted, cursing me as she went.

Impatience and tension remained when she returned, so I pulled Brodie aside.

"Here's some insight for you, Brodie. Life is not fair, you're right. None of it is. There's no formula. So you can sit and do nothing and blame everybody else for whatever happens to you or you can put forth some effort to learn. You can make a life for yourself. It just takes time, moment by moment, battle by battle. Get past the world-is-against-me thinking. The world doesn't care."

Who does care? I wondered as she broke down and tears filled her eyes.

We had a civil conversation about her behavior and a future with Damon. And the last three days of school Brodie was absent.

⊶⊷

Another school year commenced and Brodie was absent from the first day of her second year as a junior.

I phoned Uncle Art. His words shook me.

"Brodie's in a juvenile detention center for a drug violation and carrying a concealed weapon. She'll receive her education at that facility."

I stared at my office walls thinking of what Brodie must stare at every day knowing she was no longer a part of the music.

TIME EXISTED

There was something unsettling about Tracie's behavior that chilly September morning. She shuffled into class twenty minutes late, then laid her head on the desk and slept.

When I woke her, she spewed excuses and foul words. I noticed Tracie's glassy, dilated pupils and the looseness of her uniform as she tried to sneak from the classroom but fixated on the overhead lighting and mumbled something about pink and purple swirls.

The supervisor, Mr. Stark, escorted her to the office and I rehearsed some key lines before phoning Tracie's mom, Ms. Burke. I used words like *fragile, hugs, help, drugs, love,* and *protect* but in what order or shape they came out and how they were heard, I had no clue.

Ms. Burke said, "I will leave work as soon as possible to see what is really happening. Tracie does not use drugs."

The contempt in her voice was unmistakable as she spoke through gritted teeth. I pictured the corner of her lip pulled back and upward in a sneer.

⊷⊶

Tracie returned to lab, an odor of burnt rope in her wake. Did she smoke a joint between the office and lab?

She appeared haggard and gaunt, her habit robbing her skin of luster as she fidgeted and soared to a high. Her leg bouncing became annoying to those around her as they took notes and asked questions during class. Tracie just doodled and scribbled nonsense.

I asked Tracie to my office. Her inability to concentrate and her memory lapses concerned me. At mention of her grades, she exploded.

"It's none of your concern. You're just like my mom, all up in my business," Tracie screamed in an uncontrollable tirade. "Telling me to do my homework and asking about my friends, and refusing to let me go where I want. And she says it's all about keeping me safe. NO. She doesn't trust me so you just butt out too."

She started talking incessantly and became agitated about a homework assignment. She grabbed her chest, staggered, and collapsed to the floor, her arms and legs twitching. Just then, Ms. Burke and Supervisor Stark entered my office. He quickly phoned 911, hoping help would arrive soon.

⇒+ +⇐

Nine days later our principal delivered some sad news.

"Over the weekend the police found Tracie in a hotel room with two men. They were all drinking, and, you know, Tracie is underage. They also confiscated heroin, cocaine, amphetamines, and Benzedrine. All those in the room tested positive for cocaine, and Tracie's now in juvenile detention."

My office phone rang later that morning, and I heard Ms. Burke's desperation. She spoke so rapidly I missed parts.

"Tracie had to go to court. I can't afford an attorney, so she has a court-appointed one."

I asked, "How did the case turn out?"

"These prosecutors are going to ruin her life. And she fell right into their hands—cursed me, you, the school, cops, lawyers, and the system," Ms. Burke cried. "I hardly recognize her anymore, she's become so dark."

"Is she home or still in juvenile detention?" I asked, but all I heard were the tears and sorrow as she hung up. I was saddened by Tracie's behavior but not surprised.

I believe a time existed when Tracie sparkled with life—a time before I knew her, a time before illegal drugs.

PART FOUR

a time to cast away stones, and a time to gather stones together;
a time to embrace, and a time to refrain from embracing...

Ecclesiastes 3:5 ESV

SEPTEMBER'S NEW KEYS

My new classroom and lab was narrow and long with three doors of escape for students—one in the front, another in the middle, and a top secret one in the rear. I felt like I needed an orientation on how to instruct twenty-eight females and keep watch on three doors too.

"Tell them not to use the back door," my supervisor said.

During the first week I noticed four of my students slip out the hidden door a few minutes before the dismissal bell rang. I didn't yet know all the students' names but I reported the escape and they received detention, and I was directed to watch more diligently. So I enlisted the help of my across-the-hall colleague, Peter Gomez.

Peter became my hall monitor and quickly realized that Harriet was the ringleader. She incited the prisoners held captive in my lab. Nonetheless, in last five minutes of class, Harriet escaped unnoticed and my supervisor was unhappy with me again.

"Have you no control? Do you not know what you're doing?" she taunted.

Harriet withdrew from school and returned to her home school. The other three failed my lab and returned to their home schools.

The next week another student, Erica, wore pink print pajama pants to lab. I cocked my head to the side, annoyed at her inappropriateness. Before I could address the issue, my supervisor, with her over-the-glasses look, snatched Erica from my class. But Erica refused to change clothes so she was sent home. The next day she wore slippers and was sent home again. And the following day she showed off her nose ring.

Self-centered or rebellious? I wondered.

I wandered to her desk. "I like the nose ring, Erica," I said, "but do you remember it's not permitted during school hours?"

Her face softened for a brief second.

I no sooner had uttered the words than the principal was by my side, seemingly upset with me, and Erica was whisked away.

Overnight Erica's hair turned bright blue. The supervisor scooped Erica up before she had even made it to my class. After three days of detention and ten days of normal, Erica walked into class with a cup of coffee from a fast-food joint. The supervisor's eagle eye missed the cup and I ignored it.

The following week, though, Erica was caught red-handed with two cups of java—one for her and one for me. Kindhearted. But I was the only one with that opinion. Erica earned a three-day suspension. And this rebellious behavior and my reprimands continued until she graduated in the spring.

⇥ ⇤

Three years later Erica appeared at my office door after school. I barely recognized her. Light brown hair framed her delicate face. Straight bangs made her eyes dance, and I could spot no piercings or tattoos. It was the two cups of java that gave her away. She handed me mine and gave me a hug.

"Erica, how great to see you! You look well."

"I'm in school now. Wanna be a rad tech. I had to get rid of the piercings and quit dressing so punk. Guess I'm growing up like you told me I needed to," she said with a grin. "Anyway, I just had to let you know what I'm doing with my life."

I smiled as she left and thought of Kalen and his keys.

SLUSH

When I arrived, Parker and Cindy stood in my office doorway fidgeting. Cindy waved for me to hurry, her arms spinning about like a windmill.

"Renee stole the blue silk blouse my grandma sent me from China out of my classroom locker," Cindy said.

"And your locker was locked?" I asked.

She stared at me with her mouth hanging open.

"Cindy?"

"No," she said sheepishly. "We want you to search her before she leaves the room."

"I won't do that," I said, sounding a bit edgy with my stomach slushing.

Parker chimed in. "Renee has had sticky fingers since grade school. She still steals our pencils and gets stuff out of the girls' purses. I even found her in my backpack tryin' to steal my Colt's football jersey. One day Renee elbowed Sammie as she walked by her in the locker room. Then she knocked her down. Good thing Sammie laughed it off. You never saw it 'cause we pulled the curtains."

Of course they did, I thought, and that caused my insides to flip again.

"Yeah, she steals our lunches, too, and even takes our makeup," Cindy said. "I've found her with my lipstick and eye shadow before. Of course, she said her mom bought it for her. That's a lie."

"All this is true," Parker substantiated. "She's a thief and a liar. And just so you know, she cheats on her tests. We all know it. Just watch her the next time you give us a test."

I felt like upchucking at that point, but there was no time for that.

"Did you see her steal your blouse, Cindy?" I asked.

"No."

Once class began I asked if anyone knew anything about the theft of Cindy's blouse.

Renee was the first to answer. "Well, I can tell you I didn't do it. It's terrible to know that someone in here is a thief. Poor Cindy. That blouse is a gem and means so much to her."

Then she walked over to Cindy and gave her a quick hug.

At lunch I found Mr. Hough, the assistant principal, and recounted my knowledge of the theft. I also noticed that none of my students sat with Renee. No one sat with Renee. Or was it Renee who did not sit with them? Renee shot daggers from her deep piercing eyes, then turned away with an evil smile.

After the students were gone for the day, Mr. Hough informed me that he'd found the silk blouse in Renee's hallway locker.

"I'm going to call her mother now and Renee will be dealt with first thing in the morning," he said.

An hour before school began the next day, Renee and her mother, Mrs. Conlin, arrived in my classroom.

Renee looked nervous, almost scared, and acted as if chewing off the end of her finger would help. She drew a little closer to her mother and looked as though she wanted to bolt.

I made eye contact with her and smiled softly. Mrs. Conlin stared at the floor, as if to melt into the cracks.

The moment of truth had finally come for them. Over the next hour Renee and her mother shared the story of struggle and shame.

Renee spoke first, releasing years of pain. "I was raped."

Mrs. Conlin hesitated. "Renee's been abused and raped."

"It was Jay, my older brother," Renee blurted out. "I always felt like it was my fault. I mean, I was thirteen. I thought I was the only girl who was raped."

"And I thought we could work through this together, that she wouldn't need any other help," Mrs. Conlin said.

"None of this was your fault, Renee," I assured her. "You have value in this life."

Renee nodded.

"She started lying, stealing, and separating herself from her friends," Mrs. Conlin said. "I couldn't stop her dating all sorts of unsavory characters, if you get my drift. I guess that's my fault, so I've decided to transfer Renee to another school."

"Mom, Jay still lives with us, and you know he still abuses both of us and rapes me."

"What?" I said. "You both need some serious help from a counselor or psychologist."

"Jay is my son, my first born. I can't just throw him out," Mrs. Conlin cried.

"Mrs. Conlin," I said, "you know I have to report this to the authorities."

Her reply was quick. "Oh no, you won't, you can't. Mr. Hough said he wouldn't because Renee is leaving the school, and Renee will get help somewhere. We'll figure that part out."

"I'm sorry, I can't accept that. Jay needs to leave and both of you need help. I will call Child Protective Services."

Mrs. Conlin's volume rose, and the slush in Renee's life gushed out in a muddy blitz as she chewed her lower lip. But there was more in Renee's eyes—something unreadable and detached, something

I would never know. Having seen that look before, I wondered if she had ever entered the fun world of make-believe—a little girl's world of pigtails, dolls, and tea parties.

I stood my ground and phoned Child Protective Services but never learned the outcome.

A PERFECT STORM

"Turn to page 227 in your workbooks," I said. "You are to complete the first six pages before you leave today and then practice the skills on the following pages."

The moans and groans arose as if the students were overburdened. I gave my usual smile and ignored them. Then, without warning, Bryce swept his arm across his desk, sending his books and papers into the air, and he jumped up and ran around the room yelling obscenities.

"Open your books, kid," Bryce began with loose words and thoughts. "I know your plot. There are needles in the books. They hurt me and make me bleed. I heard you planning to go to the park and kill the flowers. No, no. Run in the clover and green grass but I won't kill flowers." Pause. "Do you hear those school buses? They left me. Took the newspaper boy. Boy, boy. No, no, no. The school bus ran over, over, over, the clover, clover, clover." He laughed.

Bryce continued his repetition, laughter, and rants for a good ten minutes before he propped against the storage closet, slid down the door, and sat on the floor. He proceeded to stare at the wall, mumbling to the unseen.

The students stayed put, but little effort was put into their assignment with their attention on Bryce.

⚊⚋⚊

The first day I met Bryce, he had blurted out, "Hey lady, I'm Bryce and I don't want to be here. I hate this lab." He then wandered the room, picking up supplies from the work tables and throwing them to the floor.

I walked toward him, extending my right hand. "Welcome to my lab and to this class. Perhaps I can change your mind. Now please take your seat in the front row. I saved it just for you."

He was a bit reluctant but he followed my request. Over the next three hours, Bryce doodled rather than working and spoke not a word to other students. He never even faced his classmates and no one sat on either side of him.

He developed a habit of not shaving a small round spot under his lower lip. I said nothing, thinking the supervisors would correct this school violation, but they said nothing. Day after day he stomped into the room and slammed his books on his desk, loudly declaring, "I still don't like it here."

And each day I greeted him with, "Bryce, I'm glad you're back. Maybe today we will find your interest."

I informed the school counselors, the administration, and my colleagues of his behavior. I phoned his home and left messages. But my words turned out to be lost.

He only glared. The other students refused to work on projects with him and did not talk with him. In fact they scooted their desks out of his range.

Bethany even whispered to me, "We are afraid of him. We all think he's crazy."

I understood and couldn't make sense of Bryce's behaviors, and he refused to see a counselor.

That evening I turned the television on to the Weather Channel. The meteorologist was talking about high-pressure systems and how low-pressure systems cause thunderstorms. And something clicked. These forces gather to create a perfect storm—a storm where anger loses control, fear confronts paranoia, and delusion meets reality.

The next morning Bryce drummed his fingertips on the desk.

"Please don't tap the desk," I asked. "I know you don't mean to but it distracts the others."

He raised only his eyes to me and drew his index finger across his throat. His breathing was heavy and deep. I reported this to administration, hoping I was heard, but Bryce remained in my lab. There was no effort to move him to the juvenile psychiatric center or even place him in another lab—one he may like or be more suited to. And his parents made no effort to seek a psychiatric assessment.

Supervisor Carpenter told me, "Bryce would not be safe in a lab with heavy equipment like welding, auto mechanics, or carpentry. I can't put him in the graphic arts, the business program, or childcare. This is the best place for him and you can handle him. Come on, work with me here."

I replied, "He's not passing my lab. Besides he won't be safe with patients. And what about my students' safety?" I had no clue whether Supervisor Carpenter ignored my warnings or if his hands were tied by parental decisions and law.

I had learned during clinical nursing that the little signs do not get recorded. They are insignificant except that they are not normal. As a collective, though, little abnormalities mean something. But by the time little signs are evaluated, they characterize the presence of something else, a specific loss of function.

⊷⊶

Bryce remained seated against the storage closet door. His bowl haircut framed his face and bangs swept across the tops of his eyebrows. His eating habits had added weight to his small five-foot-eight bone structure. Since I had never seen him smile, his dull brown eyes had remained distant and hazy.

I circled the room, checking work in progress and then joining Bryce on the floor.

For a fleeting few minutes, Bryce spoke coherently.

"I like to wrestle with my dad and brothers until I hurt them. I have five older brothers, ya know. A few weeks ago, I threw my brother into a table and it broke." He smiled, flexed and relaxed his arm muscles, and made a fist as each freckle on his arm bounced.

He went on talking about his brothers and the fights they had and about his dad and how strict he was.

"Bryce, you haven't told me about your mom," I said.

The hair on his arms bristled. "We all got rid of her. That's what makes me strong, Dad says. Don't need no woman 'round. And Dad gets what he wants, if ya know what I mean."

"And how is it at home without your mom?"

He turned and looked at me. "Why are you looking at me? You look like a horse. You know they made me do that, play Ring Around the Rosie. They had pockets full of flowers, dead ones. Don't you do that or I will have to leave."

I tried to intercede with reality, but he talked incessantly, twirling hair at the nape of his neck.

"I heard what he said to you," Bryce continued, "that the man will stab me. Pain. Pain. Hit. Hit. I won't. I won't. I won't. No. No. No."

He slapped and beat himself in the head, swatted at the air, then ducked his head as if pantomiming an attack from another person. He stood, opened the storage closet door, and hurled books, notebooks, lunch bags, and papers to the floor. One book hit me on the leg and another walloped my head. I rolled over quickly to get out of the way and motioned for Taylor to phone the main office for help.

Bryce chased his unseen attacker. "Get you. Get you! Get you..."

He created his path, pushing over empty desks, chairs, and any equipment in his way. The students scattered as he babbled ugly, nonsensical words. I positioned myself between the door to the hallway and him and motioned for my students to leave the room.

I called his name four times before he turned to me. I smiled. "Bryce, do I upset you?"

His response was quick. "I hate. I hate. I hate you! But wait. They took my waddleshmoo. I need my waddleshmoo." He looked to his left and talked to someone I did not see. "I won't do it! No! Don't touch me. Where's my waddleshmoo?"

He turned back to face me and took his shirt off, squaring his shoulders in a fight pose. His face was red, sweat dripped from his brow, and his body shook with tension. He began to remove the belt from his pants.

When Supervisor Carpenter arrived Bryce grabbed and punched at him. An unwilling Bryce departed with him, leaving the students and me in the aftermath of the storm. We sat in silence for the remaining time we had in class. I would never understand what must have been coursing through his mind.

⟨⟩

In a dark corner of Bryce's house, tucked in back of his closet, was a secret door—one that only he knew existed. The dull rough door led to a narrow closet with a lower ceiling, the private world of Bryce. It was his place to hide from the storms of Dad and five older brothers, the web he was ensnarled in. He tried not to be entangled in their callous words and their fists. This tiny space was his haven from the chickens, vermin, and roaches that wandered the house—a haven from the stench of uncleanliness. He hid from the voices, the ones only he heard. But the voices found him.

⋙⊹⊹⋘

The following Monday, I headed straight to Supervisor Carpenter's office, where I found local law enforcement officers. They informed me that Bryce tried to knife his dad and brothers over the weekend. Officers had found blood splattered about the kitchen and the hallway leading to Bryce's room. Dad and the brothers had bloody slashes on their arms and hands and were treated by EMTs at the scene.

But where was Bryce? None of the officers had been able to find him until forty-five minutes later when the officers located his secret door. They sent him to a juvenile center for psychiatric evaluation. They found no key for entry into this hidden space, which Bryce considered his only safe space.

That weekend a storm of activity had overwhelmed Bryce. In his private place he remained safe and alone with his voices, in his space of shelter—his believed safety—sweeping him into oblivion.

⋙⊹⊹⋘

I never learned if what Bryce had told me about his family was true. And I never learned what happened to Bryce after his psychiatric evaluation or what diagnosis he was given. The students never asked about him nor did anyone else.

BIRDIE

I saw Kayleigh and her son in the office after school. She walked toward me, threw her arms around me, and asked to talk. We headed to my office with her five-year-old, Jared, who scurried in front of us with little footsteps.

In the lab Kayleigh found her old desk and rubbed the top with her hand before sitting down as if she were still a student.

Kayleigh told me that a man had abused her mother.

"He beat her with a belt, punched her with his fist, and banged her head into the wall."

"What did you do?" I asked.

"I ran and hid in my room with my baby doll, Birdie. Sometimes I'd peak through the keyhole. Birdie and I kept all the secrets in our house an' I still have her. She's really the only friend I have."

"May I ask who he was?" I inquired.

"Some old man who came home with Mommy once, then stayed."

Jared ran between my office door and the hospital bed tucked in the corner. He jumped up on the bed and used it like a trampoline, and before I could say anything, he tumbled to the floor. He screamed and cried and arched his back in pain and irritability. Kayleigh gathered him in her arms like a rag doll and left without a word.

I remembered Kayleigh as a tall, lanky junior with tousled mid-length black hair and broad hands with thick-scarred knuckles. Her hands had seemed rigid and unbreakable and the routine cracking of her knuckles had been irritating. Tattoos were scattered about her arms and chest and a black chain draped her neck.

Three weeks passed before Kayleigh returned to talk with me. She knocked on my door at 4 p.m., just as I was ready to leave.

"She was an alcoholic. I guess Dad wouldn't marry her an' she started drinkin' more and goin' to bars. I never knew him. He got shot in a bar fight. Anyway, Mommy couldn't make ends meet, so she brought men home. They'd take drugs and get drunk, an' eventually she got hooked on heroin. I was little and her bedroom was always noisy and off limits. It was a time before I knew what existed in life. She's in prison now for twenty-five years."

"Are you able to visit her?" I asked.

Kayleigh smiled and made a guttural sound. "Nope. She doesn't wanna see me."

Nine weeks later Kayleigh knocked on my front door. How did she know where I lived and where was Jared? Dark circles under her tiny eyes and tangled, unwashed hair covered her gaunt face and rumpled T-shirt.

We sat on the front porch in the warm afternoon radiance. She seemed detached.

"I can't sleep or eat. I get nervous and irritated with Jared. A friend has him for a few weeks. I don't want to hurt him."

"I wondered where he was," I said, but she ignored me.

"I didn't hear the old man come down the hall an' didn't know he was outside my room 'til he kicked the door in. He picked me up, ripped Birdie out of my arms, and threw her on the floor. My only friend. That's when I screamed and cried and kicked him. He slapped me in the head an' I cried more. Up close, his face was unbearably large and ugly. His nose was flattened and covered with little bumpy paths of broken blood vessels. I'll never forget that face."

She took a sip of lemonade and a short silence followed as I digested her words. She thought her door kept everyone out. It was not safe to let the outside in. Maybe if she whispered to Birdie, she wouldn't hear them scream. She told Birdie her sorrows and fears. Birdie always listened and never talked back or gave her bruises. A five-year-old pouty lip tucked into a frown helped fight tears because tears were weakness. Maybe if she hugged Birdie she would fall asleep and it'd all go away. Kayleigh couldn't reach Birdie.

"He didn't say nothing, jus' pulled me down the hall. Mommy was screamin' at him. She was high and stood behind the couch with a bloody nose. Then the cursing and yelling stopped 'cause this old man shoved a tube of cold metal in my mouth and glared at Mommy. I remember not bein' able to breathe and tastin' blood, then hearin' a click. Mom disappeared behind the couch an' I heard her bawlin'. He threw me on the floor an' I hit my head really hard. I was too scared to even cry. The next thing I knew I was crawlin' back to hug Birdie. Her arm was ripped and the stuffin' was fallin' out and her pretty face was all torn. All I could do was cry and hug her. Later I fixed her with Band-Aids hidden under my bed."

"This must be hard to talk about, Kayleigh," I said to comfort her.

"Yep. I think I better leave now." She put her lemonade down on the side table between us and stood to leave. Kayleigh placed her hand on the car door and peered through the window, then turned toward me and said, "You know, my life's screwed up."

I nodded as she walked back to the porch and sat down.

"I didn't see what happened next," she said after a few minutes, "but Mommy told me the old man drug her outside, beat her with his belt, and tried to shoot her. He told her he was gonna kill me, too, and maybe even make her watch. Mom showed me her scars. I guess a neighbor called the cops, but before they got there, the old man shot himself in the head. No loss. Mommy went to a rehab place and I went to a foster home, one of twelve over thirteen years. I waited but Mommy never came back for me an' then I found out she went to prison."

Kayleigh wrapped her fingers around the chair arms so tightly her knuckles turned white.

"I never felt good enough for anything or anyone," she said. "If anybody tried to help me, I gave them lip or beat 'em up. They told me I'm quick to anger, but you knew that. Too bad. I'm no different than he was."

We emptied our lemonade glasses as evening shadows covered the front porch and a chill moved in.

"Would you like to join us for dinner tonight, Kayleigh?" I asked.

I thought her face softened for a moment but then her image hardened again and she left, her direction unclear and her motives unknown.

TANTRUMS

"Haley, come into my office. It's time for your nine-week conference," I said.

I reviewed Haley's enthusiasm to learn, her zeal for perfection, her impatience with others, and her frustration with herself. Then we looked at her class assignments, presentation grades, and test scores before moving on to skills.

"Haley, you practice twelve times with only me as an observer. Remember, you are to use me when you require help, if you do not understand, or when you are ready to complete the particular skill to standard." I saw an erosion but I carried on. "Haley, you've earned a C this nine weeks."

Somewhere a seawall cracked and crumbled into pieces, the flood of tears drenching her cheeks as she struggled to breathe. She ran from my office and staggered around the room like a pinball, slamming into desks and pushing books to the floor before throwing her body down and banging her hollow fists against the lockers.

Haley's entire appearance had changed, veiling the pretty behind this fit of bad temper. Fire flared within her eyes and her classmates stood dazed, trying not to laugh.

She wept and bawled. Ten minutes later I beckoned and she crawled from the locker room to the front of the classroom and curled up on the floor beside me. What am I witnessing?

"Haley, please stand," I said. "I will phone your mother, then you and I will go to the administration area where your mother can pick you up and take you home for the day."

On our sluggish walk down the hallway, I asked Haley to explain her agitation and anxiousness, but I got no response.

"Are you afraid of failing? Rejection?" I asked.

Still no answer.

Haley's mom, Mrs. Kaiser, arrived a half hour later.

"Now, young lady," she said, "you tell me the truth. What happened?"

Haley filled the air with anything but the truth. "She embarrassed me in front of all my classmates...called me a failure...said no one likes me...wants me to change labs. And she gave me a C. That's how mean she is. Oh Mommy, it's awful."

Character flaw? Spoiled? Pressured to be perfect. Am I in the real world?

Mrs. Kaiser looked sharply my way and leaned over the reception counter so close to me that I saw my own reflection in her eyes. She pointed her finger in my face, demanding, "Change her grade to an A or I will report you."

"No. I will not because a C is what she earned."

"You will be sorry."

"Mrs. Kaiser, Haley is not failing. I believe she needs to put a little more time into her studies," I explained.

Haley was an only child and Mrs. Kaiser was divorced when Haley was two years old. She never knew her father. Haley's outside class projects were always perfect. And if she did not get her way, she threw a tantrum until she did. But that would not work with me or in life.

Things calmed for a few weeks and then one morning, Haley's eyes swelled with tears.

She asked, "Didn't you grade this wrong?"

"I don't believe so, but let me check it. The error lies here, Haley. All you needed to do was enter—"

"Mommy is the only one who helps me. You pick on me," she cried, turning her face from me, unable to contain the tears.

In a panic she hurried away to the locker room to hide imperfection in perceived normalcy. The tantrum about everyone wronging her continued for twelve minutes. I let the outburst proceed because if I sent her to the office, the secretary would phone her mother.

Two days later another crisis sprung up when I had Haley repeat chest compressions for the tenth time and refused to pass her CPR skills. That time I phoned her mother, who came again to take Haley home.

"It's your fault she's not able to do these CPR skills," Mrs. Kaiser spat.

I wondered if these tantrums were isolated to my lab until I heard violent retching in the hallway one afternoon. Haley was on the floor, heaving and crying in pain that she had to vomit.

"I'm so sick. Get help. Get my mommy."

Mr. Hernandez walked out of his room and said, "She has a math test to take but said she isn't ready to take it. She has known about the exam for a week. This is just another one of her acts."

Similar events occurred through the year, frazzling every nerve in my body. They were scenes I will never understand, imperfections everyone else's fault. And Haley's mother only reinforced her need for perfection, driving her on an aimless course and forgoing any attempt at direction or control.

THE CIRCLE MAKER

Yvonne raised her hand. "What's an orgasm?"

There was no possible way to conceal my shock. Students exchanged wide-eyed glances and moved about to hide their laughter.

"I will talk with you in my office later," I said. "Let's focus on today's lesson."

Yvonne nodded, then after class raced out of the room as if escaping a fire.

Two days later Yvonne doodled in her notebook and talked to herself and the empty chair to her left rather than taking notes. She nodded, laughed, and thrusted her arms outward like she was hugging someone before rocking in her chair and falling asleep.

I talked with her after class and noticed a detachment in her. My words on inappropriate behavior and sleeping in class were met with laughter and she walked out, mumbling to herself.

As the days passed, Yvonne blurted out more inappropriate words and questions, ignored classroom lectures, and did not participate in lab demonstrations. Disagreements between Yvonne and classmates and teachers also escalated and rapid shifts occurred in conversation.

"My sister is really cool, but my mom always gets angry at me," she said. "I never get angry because I love everybody. I love pictures of naked men. Do you? My cat loves me. Cats are so cuddly and cute. They don't like dogs. Dogs are man's best friend. Friends can be enemies. My friend is an enemy of the school."

Later I heard the loosening of any connective thoughts and even words.

"I need to study for your bubbywub tomorrow. I should read that wakidloo but would rather have schmucky."

I collected my students' notebooks to evaluate their work and examined Yvonne's first. Images of sinister faces and demons and bats with men's faces and sketches of intimate body parts labeled with obscene names littered the pages. But more horror was to be seen: drawings of sex acts and little girls who watched and performed them while the beasts laughed. There were no classroom notes. Words splashed on pages, making disjointed sentences with scrambled thoughts, and writings wound in concentric circles on the pages— meaningless terms in childlike penmanship. Page after page I read on as the obscene turned to shame. The words *Dad, Mom, me, hurt,* and *cry* stockpiled on one page, then appeared on each sheet of paper.

Is this some sort of plea for help? I struggled to understand these simple markings and complicated emotions written by a child.

The after-school yogurt in my stomach began to churn. I took a deep breath and phoned Yvonne's mother. When she answered, I fought to find the words.

"I wanted to talk with you about Yvonne. I've been noticing—"

She interrupted. "What's she done this time?"

"She has done nothing. I'm quite concerned about her obsession with—"

"Look, I am her foster mom. I only took her in to give her a place to sleep and eat, and all she's done is cause havoc in our home. I told her, one more call from the school, one more problem, and she's leavin' here."

"It seems her problems are deep, deeper than someone untrained and unskilled can help," I said. "Of course, we here at school will help all we can, but I think she needs your love and support along with proper counseling with someone she trusts. I can recommend someone I think—"

For the third time she dismissed my perspective.

"Oh, she's in counseling with the fourth counselor. She wouldn't listen to the first two and the last one, she just refused to go. Child Protective Services got her this woman and she's going now, not that it's doin' much good."

A few moments of awkward silence passed.

"I'll call you again in a couple of weeks to check her progress. Please be patient with her," I pleaded.

She moaned and hung up.

There was no change in Yvonne, no visible progress. Students avoided her no matter how I created lab groups. They thought she was weird and scary and I couldn't convince them otherwise. She blindsided them with questions about sex, and they smiled at each other when she hallucinated and laughed when she showed them her notebook. My conversations with Yvonne were to no avail, either, but Child Protective Services and the school administration felt she needed to stay in my lab because she trusted me.

"She would manage better in a juvenile psychiatric facility, a place where she can receive intense, proper care," I argued. But that was not an option.

Yvonne's foster mother, Jane Stevens, introduced herself and sat down across from me in my office. Her cheekbones were high and mid-length mousy brown hair sprung in all directions covering her narrow eyes and pointy nose.

"Yvonne does have a mental illness and I don't want her labeled," she said. "It is unrecorded. She refuses to open up about her parents. Her dad was shot in a gang fight roughly three years ago and her mom's in prison. I doubt she ever wanted Yvonne."

She sighed as I watched history shroud her.

"Her mom is my sister and she's part of the gang and does drugs and whatever else they want. The gang, the drugs, they'll never let my sister out of their grasp. She's trapped. I took Yvonne in about four months after her dad was gone. The things that child saw and was forced to do…well, it's horrifying. I am trusting you not to tell."

She thought it was a secret rather than a burden.

"Your work in lab's too hard for Yvonne. Lighten it up some so she won't fail again. She's almost eighteen and needs to be on her own, making her own decisions."

I showed her Yvonne's writings and completed assignments, the few she'd turned in. And I shared her classroom questions, behaviors, and sloppy appearance.

"She refuses to take her medicine. I guess she doesn't like how it makes her feel," Mrs. Stevens said.

I didn't talk with Mrs. Stevens again until a month later when she showed up unannounced.

After several minutes of sniffles and tears, she spoke. "I-I don't know where to begin. My daughter, Caitlyn…I found her diary. Caitlyn. We call her Cate. It means purity, you know. I guess I'm not here to talk about her. It's Yvonne. She's beginning to have influence over Cate. There's a lot of things Cate wrote about sex in her diary, things I know she's too young for. She's only eleven. She hates me for havin' Yvonne in our house but then she says she loves Yvonne and wants to be like her. I just wanted to help my sister and Yvonne. I've called Child Protective Services and they're goin' to find other foster parents. I have to protect my daughter."

Yvonne was left to spin and weave more delicate and transparent concentric circles over time, beginning four days later when she moved to her new foster family, a new program, and a new school.

WOUNDED BEAR

Aubrie threw herself into the chair, her face burning and her eyes glaring into empty space. She leaned the chair back on two legs and rolled her fingers into fists. Her words stripped my flesh.

"So you want to know about me, my life? What a joke! Life's a bitch, ya hear? My drunken brother beats me up all the time, but I got the best of him last night. He's got a shiner. My parents hate me. The end. I ain't tellin' you no more."

Wounded bear raged. I backed away and moved on with class. But Aubrie's attitude persisted. And anger reinforced her behavior.

Every day awakened a new nightmare. That morning she thundered into the classroom, her left fist pounding her right hand. Foul language gushed.

"He always picks on me, jus' like everybody else. My brother, I hate him. I'll kill him. I'll kill him," she said.

The words ricocheted off the walls. My shock mirrored the students' and Aubrie aimed a fierce look my way. Her world was shattered, her soul was wounded, and her bitterness drew me in for another bite.

I forced myself to stand beside Aubrie as she trudged through her assignment, startling at sudden noises and unforeseen movements. She stepped backward, her frantic den of wrath giving me pause. Should I run? Or is it she who will run? Does she trust anyone? Does she trust herself?

"I hate you. You can't make me talk," she spewed at me, her hostility escalating.

She clawed at her book bag, threw her book at the wall, and slung pencils to the floor before kicking and punching the classroom door.

"It's all your fault," she screamed as I approached. Nose to nose with me, the wounded bear struck. "I hate you an' the bus driver an' my brother an' my parents. I hate 'em all."

My heart raced and my brow sweat until administration arrived to escort her out.

⋯⊹⊹⋯

Together, Aubrie and I planned her nursing home clinical experience. I paired her with a capable and reliable student, hoping that, in time, Aubrie would function on her own, controlling her anger by stepping outside and taking deep breaths while gathering her thoughts. Maybe, just maybe, Aubrie could taste success then and learn to make life decisions.

⋯⊹⊹⋯

Maple Gait was fifty minutes from the school. Trees, bushes, and a fountain covered the grounds and lovely spring tulips, daffodils, and irises swayed in the spring breeze.

The staff at Maple Gait embodied the warmth toward and love of residents this clinical was to instill in my students. The residents were clean and the facility smelled fresh. Despite that, residents wore shirts where the buttons and buttonholes baffled each other.

As we passed residents' rooms, some waved and a trickle of ladies' perfume permeated the hallway. Their faces showed little emotion, though, due to disease, medication, or maybe sorrow. Residents anticipated fading into the shadows as life left them a bit at a time.

Students saw the camouflage of the flowers and realized that spring remained at the doorstep as residents whisked them into an unknown time. Students were assigned residents who required a high level of care, and they struggled with communication skills as they assisted each resident with basic personal care needs.

Students journaled their practice experiences daily, writing about what they learned as well as struggles and fears, and then we shared and discussed solutions. A tenderness surfaced in Aubrie when she joined in the discussions.

As the days passed, Aubrie began spending extra time with residents—chatting and wheeling them to the lounge or outdoor patio and buying them gifts and things they needed. And Aubrie's classmate, Tina, told me that Aubrie visited residents after school too. The staff at Maple Gait reported Aubrie holding the residents' hands, hugging them, and kissing them on the forehead. And she even visited on weekends. The families, residents, and staff enjoyed her visits and knew her by name.

⊶⊷

When the state board of nursing sent students' results on the nurse aide test, I was thrilled that Aubrie, Tina, and Mary Jo had passed. We celebrated with applause and a pizza-sized cookie.

Aubrie approached me afterward with a bear hug and thanked me.

She started work as a nurse aide at Maple Gait in June. It was a short walk from home, so she needn't rely on anyone to get there.

―――

Three years later I took my seat in the oversize auditorium for the state board of nursing conference. At the podium was a bulky man, the first speaker of the day—an attorney. I struggled to decipher his words as they rumbled through the conference center but made out something about the first state-tested nurse aide to be dismissed. His PowerPoint clarified everything—city, facility, crime, school of training, and identity: Aubrie.

It was an ambush. I filled with dread. The other state nurse aide instructors heard every word. Many leaned forward and stared at me. I was eaten alive, slithering in my seat with nowhere to hide. I searched for an eject button under the arm of my chair but all I found was gum.

―――

I phoned Aubrie.

"Yep, I threw bath water over his face and tried to choke him because he's a dirty old man who grabbed me in the crotch. He thinks he's so special because he's some kinda big shot. I screamed at him too. Too bad somebody saw me. I ain't got my job and I'll never be a nurse aide again. And just because I told you this doesn't mean I like you and I'm done talkin'."

Click. I camped in my chair, wondering if she had a passion for belligerence.

―――

Two years later I received a letter from a mental health facility at the end of the school year. I assumed they needed new hires so I tore it open. Inside was a personal note from the social worker.

"I am sending a letter from Aubrie," it began. "You were the only person she would write to. Feel free to reply."

I flipped the page to Aubrie's writing. The raw words gave me pause.

"I've done some terrible things. I can't change that. I know I caused you problems and we did not always agree. I just wanted my own corner of the world, to be loved."

Aubrie went on, detailing how the social worker helped her write and taught her how to set limits. She liked the social worker. And Aubrie's discharge was just six months away.

"I'm owning up to what I did," she wrote. "I won't let violence get me again. I am no longer blinded by hatred. I even don't swear but say nice words. You were always kind to me. I thought maybe you liked me, but I won't get angry anymore. Thank you."

WILDERNESS

The hideaway was behind a field of fruit trees. It was a wilderness of open countryside, a gathering place and hangout for teens. Jocks, nerds, drama queens, gamers, punks, intellectuals, skaters, and the cool kids showed up until there was a crowd of thirty-four teenagers.

Music blared from speakers in the back of Artie's car, and there was a keg and plenty of other booze. Some danced, others made out, and a few took photos.

Gina made it her destination for the night, her goal to belong. She was a loner who liked anything sparkly, like elaborate silver jewelry. She stood separate from the others with her long dyed black hair, round waxen face, and smoky blue eyes. She appeared almost magical and had a vagueness that drew in boys. Yet that was not with intent.

A keg and countless booze bottles later, most of the teens left. The drama queens begged Gina to go but she remained with Brandon, one of the cool senior boys. Gina was a sophomore.

Time had lost its meaning once she realized something was wrong. She felt ill and mindless and was seeing doubles. Then her vision multiplied. She recalled counting five. The night didn't turn out the way she wanted. The blurry five took a strong hold on Gina, her clothes, and her body.

It all took place in slow motion and after it was over, Gina hung limp and collapsed under a tree among the vines in the wilderness.

Life's so precious and innocent and then it's not.

Gina was humiliated, spending the remainder of the weekend in her room rehearsing her thoughts and practicing her words—a cover-up of her behavior. There was no forgiveness of self, solely a haven of her pain.

Eighteen months had passed and Gina was now a junior in my class. Thirteen days into September, she relayed her wilderness assault to me and I saw her personal empty soul.

She saw my heart break for her in my pursed lips and wet eyes as my body tensed. I took a deep breath but could find no adequate words.

Gina patted my arm. "Don't worry. I just want you to know me," she said.

I heard control in her voice—an unshakable, unwavering control.

Eleven days later Gina returned to my office.

"I have a few stray memories," she began. "I couldn't fight it…I laid down…I couldn't tell it was the ground, it was so cold and rough…I felt lost, pain, exhaustion…I was abandoned. The whole thing seems unbelievable, savage. After a while, I quit thinking of Brandon, his buddies, and their behavior. He'd taken enough from me and was not going to get more."

Her control quivered.

My afternoon lab students filtered into the room but my thoughts of her body being yanked through darkness over rough spaces in slow motion remained.

"I told my mother, just like you said to," Gina told me a month later. "She's mad at me for not telling her when it happened. And she's mad because I won't tell her names."

Gina kept her rapist's identity concealed, cut off from what mattered that night.

Gina attended to her studies, focusing on each subject with an overwhelming desire to learn. And the following year she ran local marathons. She practiced twice a day and rode her stationary bike while studying. Her classmates encouraged her and attended her events. They believed she'd run in the Olympics one day.

Gina's gangly body and pale skin curved in over her chest and belly. At the same time she began refusing food.

"Can't stay long. Have to be at work by four o'clock. Just wanted to kill some time before I leave here," she said when she stopped in one day after school.

I expected her to tell me about her new job in the hospital dietary department. Instead Gina spoke of her counselor. Her parents had found him through a friend.

"He's a sour old man," she said. "Tall, dark-haired with thick black-framed glasses, and his jacket has patches on the sleeves. He stinks of that old musk stuff. He sits next to me and likes to pat my arm. He asks me to talk about my personal demons. How dumb. I refuse to talk to him. All he does is make me think about Brandon and what he did to me. Oops, gotta run."

A week later she returned.

"Old musk tried to hug me yesterday. I spat in his face and left. My parents said I don't have to go back. Now Dad just wants me to tell him stuff. Mom is quiet. I'm off to work."

I phoned Gina's parents.

"I wish we could have kept her innocent. We are so distraught. These memories of hers…well, she needs help. I would move mountains but I'm not sure how," her mom sobbed.

I gave her the name of a female counselor before we hung up. Then I put down my pen, dropped my head, and drew my hands through my hair to stimulate thought. But those I received were uninvited. Thoughts of abused, runaway, neglected, homeless, and poor students—all powerless and feeling hopeless—consumed me. I remembered those I couldn't help.

We all have our own wilderness—a pit hidden inside a plum, a tree hidden in a grove, or a vine hidden under a tree.

PART FIVE

a time to seek, and a time to lose;
a time to keep, and a time to cast away…

Ecclesiastes 3:6 ESV

KALEIDOSCOPE

"You've got to do something about Shelli's lies," Mr. Ferguson, the chemistry instructor known as the Professor, said.

Mrs. Jenkins, the librarian, nodded. "She's out of control. Did she say anything to you about her dad dying?"

"No," I said.

"You tell her. I can't repeat this one," the Professor said to Mrs. Jenkins.

"In Shelli's mind she drove alone over the weekend to Iowa to identify her father's body and help with his autopsy since she is in training. But she told the Professor she went to North Carolina for the same purpose."

"In training for what?" I asked, but Mrs. Jenkins ignored me.

"Well, her father died homeless and had no identifiable markings. Her words. And now Shelli's aunt is trying to get all the money and his house bequeathed to her," Mrs. Jenkins continued.

"He was homeless but has a house and money? A sixteen-year-old hired her own attorney?" I asked.

None of us had answers and Shelli only had more lies to cover the others.

I phoned Shelli's mother, Mrs. Cooper.

"Her dad did die and, well, it's not lies, if that's what you're implying," Mrs. Cooper began. "She's always embellished. Just think of it as her version of the truth."

Two weeks later Shelli told me she was flying to Arizona to sign the legal papers over the weekend.

"The court system is in session on Saturday and Sunday?" I asked.

"They're doing this for me since my aunt is so evil, so I don't miss school," she said.

"Shelli, this lying needs to stop," I pleaded.

The Professor pointed out conflicting information in her stories and Mrs. Jenkins and Shelli had a tête-à-tête, all to no avail. The more Shelli fabricated, the easier it became. She was desensitized to what she said and one story snowballed into countless deceitful words.

In the following weeks the Professor, Mrs. Jenkins, and I discovered residue of truths among the fantasies. But her lies became like the turn of a kaleidoscope—a succession of changing pretenses in a never-ending deceptive show—throughout the year.

An angry ex-boyfriend threatened Shelli. According to her, he lived in a variety of places—a different place for each person she told the tale. Our local sheriff was unable to locate him but he was found and jailed according to Shelli, then let out on house arrest. Shelli said she was assigned a protective escort, but when I asked her where he was during school, she said protection wasn't needed then.

Yellow. Two weeks later, Shelli was home alone and heard noises so she ran outside, jumped in her car, and sped away.

I thought, Does she not see each lie? Does she see the colors of truth?

Green. A few weeks later Shelli told the class that she worked as a paramedic on weekends and that she had delivered a baby the weekend prior because her fellow paramedics did not know how.

Is not eighteen years of age a requirement to be on the squad? I thought. And she followed that with a story that she alone would replace the emergency squad for football games. I challenged her story but she brushed me off.

"I'm in the band and at all events. So I'll handle all the medical issues that arise. If I need the squad I'll just call them," she said.

When I told the Professor, a former paramedic, that whopper, he laughed and called the squad. There was no record of Shelli as a volunteer and no one on staff knew her. And the last birth the squad recorded was seven years ago.

Shelli was bonded in grandeur imagery of possessing power and importance, all passé with a slight rotation.

I phoned Mrs. Cooper again.

"The students no longer believe anything Shelli tells them and she's lost credibility with her teachers as well." I paused. "I can't permit her to participate in nursing home clinicals because I cannot trust her with the patients." I went on to detail the recent lies at school.

"Oh, those clinicals will be no problem," Mrs. Cooper said. "Like I told you before, she embellishes. There was a boyfriend but they broke up. And about the baby incident, Shelli just wants to impress you."

This woman had been captured by her daughter's falsehoods and was helping her turn the kaleidoscope.

The Professor, Mrs. Jenkins, and I approached administration for a second time, but they were unable to interfere.

Gray. A week after my conversation with Shelli's mother, the ex-boyfriend resurfaced.

"He was sentenced to prison until I tell them he can be released," Shelli said confidently.

Nothing of the sort was reported in the local news. But Shelli had an answer for that too.

"The judge does not permit anyone to know for my safety."

Her detachment from reality was unhealthy.

Turquoise. The ex-boyfriend escaped from prison. Again, Shelli was in protective custody until police found him.

Blue.

"The local police are putting me through gun training and when I finish, I have permission to shoot to kill," Shelli told Mrs. Jenkins.

I phoned Shelli's mother a third time, trusting she would realize that we wanted to help.

"She told us about gun training," I said. "Shelli's embellishments are out of control. Her untruths become her truths until she has a complete break from reality. It's quite possible that Shelli has some form of mental disorder causing her to distort reality."

The silence was deeper than before. Perhaps I overstepped. What can we make of these untruths? What do we do when there's a big wall between us and help for Shelli?

Our doomed conversation ended abruptly.

Orange. The story of her father's death evolved into more patterns of lies.

Purple. Shelli told me she would not be present the last week of school. A Norwegian delegation scheduled to arrive over Memorial Day had requested Shelli's assistance in hiring security at Roller Coaster Dominion's Highpoint Inn, the massive Victorian lodging complex with verandas and a network of clear blue swimming pools on one of the Great Lakes. In summer, the lake's waves glistened as if polished. It was a dream world, an escape, a girlish fantasy.

Pink. The ex-boyfriend was still on the loose, phoning and following her.

"The police are placing me in Tennessee after graduation," Shelli claimed. "Our local college is arranging special classes for me, you know, due to my problems."

Yet she'll work up on a Great Lake? Shelli had told so many lies that she had become the lie.

White. The saga continued.

"You know, I'm executor of my father's will. And my aunt continues her legal action against me. I don't know why. All he owned was a noisy rusted car and a few old photos."

Her falsehoods created an air of mystery, so in exasperation I posed a battery of questions.

"You're not yet of legal age. Aren't you too young to be an executor?" I asked.

"Most would be, but I've been empted."

She meant exempted.

"Does your dad really have a will? I mean, I thought he was homeless."

"He just hid his valuables."

"Before, you said he had a house and money but now only a car and photos?"

"That's all the family will see."

"Monday's Memorial Day."

"This attorney will meet whenever I need him to."

"Who is your boyfriend? You didn't tell me about him."

"He's one of the EMTs I work with."

By the time I ran out of questions and realized I wasn't helping her face the truth, I wasn't hearing her tall tales. I felt devoid of truth and began to question my own sanity.

Indigo. And with another twist of the kaleidoscope, the aunt was now her grandmother, who lay in the hospital near death, so Shelli hopped on a plane to Georgia.

"I have to meet with my attorney and calm the whole family down," she said. "They're all freakin' out. Then I'll go to the hospital and tell the doctors to pull the plug."

I was speechless.

Two days later, Shelli told the Professor that her uncle had colon cancer.

"I called the family in and told them Uncle Mark is gonna die within three months," she said. "I tend to Uncle Mark in the hospital and talk to all the docs, who trust me. They don't agree on Uncle Mark's prognosis or how to help him so I told 'em what needed done. Besides, we're becoming friends. And the family does not understand medical terms so I explain it all to them. Plus, my cousin, Mary Ellen, will need a caretaker. Aunt Harriet, Mary Ellen's mother, passed away two years ago. So I'll become responsible for Mary Ellen soon."

That same day Shelli told Mrs. Jenkins that her family had appeared at the attorney and demanded a cut of her father's estate.

And the lies rolled on. Shelli was unable to start work at the hotel, but the job waited for her and her boyfriend would be in Iowa starting work at a new national burger store per the request of the head office.

The Professor, Mrs. Jenkins, and I began to lose our grip on reality amid the lies.

Shelli fixated on events that had never been. She targeted impractical events divorced from truth. But as long as she whirled her kaleidoscope, her lies would be limitless.

Shelli returned the following year, lying her way through until graduation. Her deceit only caused confusion and distancing from friends and others who tried to help her. And Mrs. Cooper refused to acknowledge that Shelli needed help, so no mental health evaluation was ever done and no professional treatment was received.

The Professor, Mrs. Jenkins, and I were unable to escape the daily barrage of her saga. All we could do was present reality to Shelli to no avail.

A few years later I dropped in a local fast-food restaurant and there was Shelli, behind the counter taking orders. Lofty tales and dreams had vanished and reality had swirled its way into her life.

SEDIMENT

In swaggered a tall but tardy Kasey wearing tight ripped jeans and an overstated Grateful Dead T-shirt. It was her seventh day being late.

Her burnt orange lips, black eyeliner, and bright blue eye shadow signaled a secretive, guarded countenance and her chocolate-brown hair, marbled with blond ends, heavy layers of drugstore makeup, and boredom-driven finger tapping gave a synthetic harshness. She appeared to be plastic poured from a mold.

After rummaging through her desk, she did her morning catwalk strut to my podium.

"My mother refuses to sign school medical forms," she said. "She becomes irritated when I ask her. I'm over eighteen, and I'll have you know, I am quite responsible."

I nodded but her haughty disdain did not go undetected.

A few weeks later I began to realize how little this all-girl class knew about the female body. They took on assignments and projects with great enthusiasm, asked questions and spent time researching, and had lively discussions that left nothing to the imagination when we began our study on pregnancy. They even did unrequired research to gain a more thorough understanding of STDs, including HIV.

I also worked on instilling images regarding the beauty of a woman, true love, and motherhood. Each question the students asked gave me the opportunity to shape the realism of sexual exploits without commitment. These young women needed to open their eyes to the beautiful people they were and develop an etched awareness of their true worth.

Several days later Kasey's crassness astounded me.

"My boyfriend's T-shirt binds his muscles like gifts wrapped for me," she said to the girls around her.

"Please stop your personal conversation and focus on our lesson," I said, perturbed.

"And his kisses make my hairs stand on end, let alone when he makes me pass out before giving in."

"This is not sex education class. To my office," I said, standing next to her with everyone's eyes upon us.

I talked with Kasey in private about her inappropriate words and thoughts and about how she had more to offer than her body, but she defended herself and argued with me.

"You will not disrupt class again to discuss your sexual exploits," I ordered.

Kasey stomped out of my office.

Two months later Kasey looked worn and stony. Dark circles under her eyes and her pale skin made her appear lifeless, and her clothes fit looser than before. She smelled like a perfume counter, an obvious attempt to hide the cigarette smoke. And she no longer associated with any of her classmates.

Time for another little conversation, I thought. But Kasey just smirked.

My numerous private and work-related conversations with Kasey over the next few months all failed. She began partaking in misdirected activities such as working at a dance club, I learned from a classmate. Adults. Dancers. Strippers.

"I knew you'd want to know," Maggie said. "She had an abortion a few months ago, then her parents kicked her out. She said it's cause she's eighteen. So she moved in with some old guy. He's thirtysomething and has her working at this dance club he owns. She works late, never gets much sleep—"

"Why didn't she tell me or someone else?" I asked, interrupting her.

"She didn't want to disappoint you. She didn't want you to leave her, too, like everyone important to her always has."

I phoned Kasey's parents but no one answered and no one returned my calls.

Driving to an event later that evening, I crossed the Bull River Bridge, replaying my discussion with Maggie in my head. It was the first time I understood the erosion along the way, peeling away layer by layer as the sediment moved toward its destination where the river channels converged at the bend. And that river moved so fast that it was taking Kasey where it was going, eroding her heart and soul as it flowed. I wondered what thought she had given to going away with the river before she jumped in.

A few days later I asked Kasey to my office.

"Kasey, you are so thin. So aloof. It's as if you're fading away before me."

She retorted with a sigh, "Uh, you're making me uncomfortable. You'll be gone from my life soon anyway. I'll be outta here."

"I'm sure you don't want to hear this, but you look unhealthy and you don't seem to care about anything. I can tell you're not eating or sleeping. I'm concerned. You need to hear all this from someone who cares about you, who you are, and who you can become."

Halfway into the one-sided conversation I noticed tears sliding down her cheeks, which she flung away as if they weren't there and then glared at me silently before leaving.

"I'm not done yet, Kasey."

She sat down, drying more tears.

"Let us help you find a different job and a new place to live," I pleaded. "Kasey, you are blind to those who want to help and deaf to those with good advice."

Still unable to cut away the hard pieces of her life, she refused to acknowledge my words.

"Life is not easy, Kasey. You already have enough difficulty. You don't want to drag that debris with you. It'll weigh you down. Take a risk to sculpt a life of happiness and joy. Or you can just walk away from me, from any help, if that is what you really want."

She stood, walked out, shut the door, and didn't look back.

CAGES WITHOUT KEYS

On the way to take Marty home, I accepted his invitation to meet and visit with his parents. Marty had missed the bus and his parents were unable to pick him up because of their farm duties.

Their modular home sat at the bottom of the hill, tucked behind an old lean-to and an older sycamore tree. I turned into the driveway and drove several yards over bumpy gravel.

Marty and I looked over the valley in its spring beauty before turning toward the two-tone faded-gray modular home. Pine trees lined the back and left side and a rusted barbed wire fence protected them. Uneven white trim edged the front and right side, and unpainted cinder blocks held the home several feet off the ground. The front yard was populated with chickweeds and dirt patches. Yellow Creek flowed over the rocks a few yards behind the trailer down through the valley.

I smoothed my white scrubs and lab coat as Marty and I ascended the three narrow steps and entered through the creaking bowed door.

Marty's parents greeted me wearing denim overalls and T-shirts. Mr. Singleton was a pleasant man, tall and slender, with an Eastern European accent. Working a farm had made him rugged and muscular. Mrs. Singleton stood in front of me but I focused on what lay behind her on the window sill.

The steel gray beady eyes and forked tongue weakened my knees. When it moved flashes of green scales dried my mouth. I scanned the area while my stomach churned. Cages—unlocked and empty cages. Are there no keys? Are the keys lost? Cages do have keys. I saw no way to escape.

I asked, "Where...where are the animals that belong in the cages?"

Mr. Singleton replied, "Oh, crawling around here somewhere."

They were on the couch, in the chairs, on the kitchen counters, and entwined around the lamps. One was curled up on the floor and one was slithering freely. And my feet were down there with them. SNAKES!

I was unable to move forward and backed against the wall, breaking into a cold sweat as I noticed the pervasive odor of rotting cabbage.

Mr. and Mrs. Singleton and Marty gaped at me, puzzled by my reaction, and I, of course, didn't understand their snake love.

Again I stammered, "Wh...when will you return them to their cages?"

According to Mrs. Singleton, "Oh, anytime they return for feeding. We give them mice, but they must be in their cages to eat."

"We release them into the wild once they've been treated and healed," Marty chimed in.

"That's nice to know," I said as graciously as I could.

Mrs. Singleton poured a cup of java for me but my hands shook and the coffee spilled. She poured another cup for me. The snakes scattered, a black one slithering over my clean white shoes.

The three other humans glided into stories of personal serpent adventures.

Mrs. Singleton announced, "Our first pet, Slinky, was our favorite snake."

They spoke of others who birthed hatchlings. My arms and legs trembled as I heard the name of each snake: Slick, Fang, and Beast. My body quaked. I was in the middle of a meltdown and crafted an excuse to leave.

I glanced at the house with geraniums in the uneven window boxes lining the trailer. Potted gerbera daisies maintained position on the three steps to the door of snake haven. An old rusty pickup truck stacked with more empty cages occupied the driveway.

Overhead, the trees rustled, waving side to side.

Two worlds, side by side: Marty's snake-filled modular home, frightful to me but loving, and a creek surrounded by beautiful country wildlife. From their perspective it was all so ordinary, natural, and remarkable. From mine, it was dreadful.

I started the van and backed out of the bumpy gravel driveway.

＊＊＊

Two days later, Marty became ill. The following day I was nauseous and had abdominal cramps and diarrhea. Marty experienced the same but he also vomited and recovered slower than I did.

Dr. Thomas grilled me.

"Where did you purchase your meat and eggs? What was your preparation? Did you cook it rare? Did you eat raw meat? Did you wash the vegetables and fruits?"

I wondered if Marty was asked the same questions.

Then, of course, my own personal hygiene came into question.

"Yes, I wash my hands after going to the bathroom and frequently when I'm cooking."

Dr. Thomas seemed stumped. But then I recalled the cup of coffee I drank at the Singletons'.

Dr. Thomas gave a humph and peered at me over the top on his glasses.

"You say they have pet snakes? Cages on the countertops? Who lives like that?" he asked.

"People who love snakes, and they are perfectly happy and healthy," I said, jumping up to run to the bathroom.

When I returned to the examining room, he said, "I have to report this to the health department, you know."

"Yes, I know. It'll cause that family heartache. They love their pet snakes and they live in the perfect place to release them back into their habitat."

I called as soon as possible to get an update on the family's health. "I had to see my doctor today," I said, "and I wanted to let you know that the health department will be visiting your home. I have salmonella. I imagine, though, that you have already been visited, since Marty is ill too."

Mr. Singleton asked, "What did you tell them? We're sure Marty has it, too, but we didn't take him to the doctor. He's just ridin' it out."

Before I could answer he hung up.

When I returned to work, Marty said, "My parents had to let all the snakes go back to the wild. Mom cried and Dad was angry."

"I'm sorry, Marty. I meant no harm, but the doctor is required to report salmonella."

I wrote the Singleton's a note of apology, but to what extent it was received I never knew.

I think often of the day I visited the Singletons and their pet snakes and wonder if we all make our own cages and if there is a key to letting us out.

OUT OF DARKNESS

During parent-teacher conferences, I met Mr. Howard, a gruff, rugged outdoorsman. At forty-nine years old, his muscles sagged as he leaned over his cane. Underlying misery lay in the crow's feet at the corners of his eyes. A lifelong hunter, camper, fisherman, and hiker who spent time with his buddies, Mr. Howard was the shell of the man he once was.

He and Vicky sat in the hallway with his son, Wade. Vicky, a young girl, wore a low-cut shirt that sat above her waistline and snug blue pants.

I said, "We should hold our conference in my office."

Wade stood and looked at Vicky. "You are not coming to my conference," he said, turning to his father. "Dad, she's not coming in here with us. She's nothing to me, just some slut you picked up at the bar. Now she tells everybody she's your Vicky."

Vicky threw herself back in the chair and stomped her foot, shaking her head and crossing her arms over her chest. She stopped smacking her gum long enough to purse her bright red lips and spew belligerent words from them.

I sat beside her and asked her to please stop cursing. I realized then that the stale pungent odor of smoke filling the hallway was emanating from her.

Wade rolled his eyes, and I helped Mr. Howard maneuver to the classroom.

An argument ensued or maybe it had begun earlier, had grown wider, and had now spiraled into this. Father and son were sucked into a tornado of heartache and loss.

Wade was tall and broad-shouldered and had blond hair and blue eyes. He paced about the classroom, circling the desks and losing his poise and easygoing mannerisms.

The girls in my class lollygagged about him and found reasons for him to help them with their assignments. They asked him to go out with them. He was kind but showed little interest. His thirsty intellect and lofty goals demanded his time be spent on studies.

Mr. Howard strummed his finger on his leg. "I was to take Vicky to a movie she wants to see. Some chick flick. I really don't wanna go," he said.

We spent over an hour together and I learned a great deal.

Two months ago Wade's mother, a pediatric physician, had run off to Arizona with a colleague. She was never legally married to Mr. Howard. Wade had an eight-year-old brother at home and their father would soon be wheelchair-bound. Wade had become his caregiver.

"I need my son to step up and be a man, take care of me and his brother. But, oh no, he can't do that. Spends too much time studyin'. That ain't gonna get him nowhere, so I got Vicky to help," Mr. Howard said.

"That's right, Dad. Come home from school and take care of a drunk. Why do you think Mom left? You've got Vicky, a nineteen-year-old. How sick. I don't even know you and I sure don't want to be seen with you anymore." Wade turned to me. "She gives him a shower and dresses him, along with anything else he wants. Ew.

Then she says she takes care of my brother. Like she's going to become his mother. And let's be real, she doesn't clean or do the wash. Our clothes lie crumpled in front of the washer until I do them. Our meals are all delivery. And I do all the cleanup while she watches TV and drinks with Dad. It's illegal. She's a scuzzball, a tramp. She wants his money and he won't listen."

Mr. Howard looked at me. "See what I mean? See what kind of son I have? Not a man."

Their voices increased in volume and intensity as they displayed their inability to have a civil conversation.

Vicky opened the classroom door, placed her left hand on her hip, and swung her hip sideward. "Done yet?"

"No, not yet," I said.

The door slammed.

The purpose of that conference was to discuss Wade's achievements in class. He had critical thinking abilities, goals and a future. I wanted Mr. Howard to meet the mathematics instructor because Wade's strength was math. But he was ready to leave and refused.

Wade stormed out, and I assisted Mr. Howard to the door and mentioned that a counselor might help his dilemma with Wade. But there was no reaction. Vicky met him at the door and they left arm in arm.

An hour later Wade returned.

"I'm moving out. I can't take it anymore," he said. "Dad's so disgusting and can't see what he's done. Mom left because he wouldn't stop drinking and running around with his buddies. That's how he reinjured his back. He was rock climbing and fell. But I have to look out for myself, just like Mom did."

Wade planned to live with his best buddy, Carter. He was moving over the weekend.

I inquired, "And your plans for college?"

"I have good grades and my GPA is 3.98. I think I'll graduate salutatorian. There should be some scholarship money. I figured you'd help me with college and other scholarship applications, and I can get loans. I've been looking for a job and think I have one at a local farm doing odd jobs."

In that moment of light and darkness, was the dream more perfect than its reality?

WHISPERS IN THE WIND

Avery screamed at Kit. Both showed snake-like eyes, pursed lips, and clenched fists. Kit threw her chair and took off across the cafeteria as if lunging over a cliff. Avery muttered swear words under her breath and took stance with her feet spread and her hands on her hips, prepared for battle in this standoff.

My colleague, Daryl, and I set out in their direction but Avery had whipped Kit to the floor and was standing over her head cursing before we made it. Avery swung a chair but Kit rolled to her left and jumped to her feet. Avery hurled the chair from over her head, but Daryl grabbed it and spun Avery around to face him. Meanwhile I wrapped my arms around Kit to stop her swinging arms and fists, then we marched both girls to the office amid the callous name-calling and cursing.

A few weeks later Avery returned from suspension, bruised and scraped. Heavy makeup covered both eyes and her gait was awkward. We talked in the custodian's closet.

"I heard his feet pounding the steps as he ran up to get me," she said. "I tried to stop him. But he swung his belt at me. I tried to duck, but he was too quick. I felt blood dripping from the side of my head and face. I couldn't believe what was happening."

I held her hand between mine.

"I hit him in the nose and laughed at him. But he was so quick, grabbing my hair and dragging me down the steps. I kicked and screamed and yelled as loud as I could. My mom heard it all but she didn't care. She just wanted him." Avery broke down and leaned on the door, drawing her arms around her chest for protection. "So he dragged me downstairs, out on the porch, and down more steps. No neighbors came to help. An' then he dragged me some more out on the gravel driveway. My side's scraped and still raw and sore. He beat me again with his belt across my back. I lost count of how many times the belt hit my back. I think I passed out. When I came to and went back inside where he and my mom were in her bedroom, well, they were having sex. It was so disgusting. Made me sick. I hated them both, but he had me first."

"Avery, what did you do?" I asked.

"I went to the bathroom and puked. I cleaned the wounds just like you showed us, bandaged them, and left the house. I hate my mom for having sex with my boyfriend."

Child Protective Services investigated. But Avery's mom denied all allegations.

"Avery is just clumsy and fell down the steps," she said.

A week later Avery grabbed Sherry, another student, and slammed her head into the table again and again. As Daryl and I approached, Avery released Sherry, but Sherry reached for a fork. Daryl calmed the crowd and I put Sherry in a bear hug and backed her into the table. She shouted obscenities and Avery stretched her arms around me trying to hit her.

Sex stayed with Avery, hibernating deep in her soul. And when it was awakened, she devoured and wrecked all life in her path.

"I was lonely and my old boyfriend posted a picture of him and Sherry holding hands an' kissing. Well, I lost it. Wanted to grab her and beat the you-know-what out of her."

Avery was given another week of suspension and another betrayal.

For three and a half months, Avery's life ran reckless and frenzied. One day she just walked out of her clinical assignment, leaving her patients. The following day she barged into my classroom wearing a cast on her left arm and bruises up and down her right arm and leg. Her face was swollen and purple.

"I'm done," she announced that day in the middle of class. "I'm going to live in Florida with a cousin and his family and live my life the way I want to."

She walked down the hallway, her cinnamon hair swinging to the bounce in her step. I closed my eyes, praying she followed footsteps that led down a peaceful beach rather than into the storm.

For six years, I received postcards from sites she had visited and Christmas cards too. I could only surmise that life was improving. And then she phoned me.

"I finished high school and became a paralegal," she said. "I love the work. It's a way I can help others, like the battered and abused women and children."

Avery had returned to marry an attorney, a man she met through her career. The wedding was charming and intimate with a few close friends. No parent ushered her down the aisle and no family stood in attendance.

"I want you to know that I only got through my sorrow during those threatening years because of you and Daryl. Both of you guided me but I just wouldn't listen. And neither of you ever gave up on me," Avery whispered to me when I hugged her in the receiving line. "I had such anger. You know, without those wounds and you guys, I would not have reached this magnificent day nor would I have faced any positive future."

Those whispers in the wind voiced a new beginning, a time of quiet.

PRISONERS OF DECAY

The odor persisted, but there was no time to scrub and clean two days in a row. The students and I poured buckets of water down the drain to handle the sewage backup odors. But the next day, the smell resurfaced.

The class and I sniffed and sleuthed and even enlisted the help of the custodian, Mac.

After school I opened both doors. Air circulated. Student chairs were stacked upon each other. Desks filled the hallway. On top of counters, beds, and remaining worktables, Mac and I clustered anything unattached to the floor and Mac guided the industrial scrubber across the tile.

The machine groaned while Mac smiled and sang, and I left for home. The room would smell with fragrance when I returned. Clean.

The next day I paused outside my classroom and ran down the list of reasons why I would not say anything in class that day. There were regulations. There was common sense. There was a derelict space filled with unsavory facts. It was the third option to avoid.

I unlocked and opened the door to air filled with the aroma of cleaning solution.

The students and I moved to the back of the lab. We stood close together, and a drain in the middle of the floor peered at us while we worked. The odor reappeared.

It wasn't the drain. Kaye stood near. Odor oozed, seeping out from her weathered skin. Cooking oil. Stale cigarettes. Dirty laundry. Dry perspiration. Sex.

"That girl stinks. Doesn't bathe," Jill said in the privacy of my office. "I can't sit by her any longer. And just to let you know, I won't partner with her either. I've been in school with Kaye since first grade. She lives with her mother and uncle in a small shanty by the lake in Horse Grove. My parents told me they don't work. They're just lazy. Kaye's mother and Kaye go nowhere. No one ever sees them except at the local grocer with the uncle. Weird, don't you think?"

I didn't know what to think, but I couldn't get my mind off Kaye's mother with her uncle. Incest? Am I hearing correctly?

A week later I taught cleanliness in the workplace. The class knew who I was talking to, and Kaye was shunned.

That day was different. Students helped out with various questions. It was not easy for me. Kaye sat with her head down and her hands in her lap. There was no eye contact.

My colleagues told me it wasn't my job. But then who should tell her?

Another week passed with no change. The infestation of odor continued. Kaye moved her right hand into her left and squeezed it like it might run away. She occupied the cushioned chair in my small office—my unsoiled chair. The room soon smelled of Kaye—foul.

I skirted the issue but in time, the discussion led to her lack of cleanliness. Defiled. Dishonored. Dejected. We talked longer and nausea overtook my body.

As I escorted her from my office, Kaye thanked me for my concern, told me I was her only friend, and hugged me. She left my office with a smile.

Her classmates stared at me. Jill scowled.

Over the next few weeks, Kaye washed and brushed her hair with little improvement. Pollution remained. So I hauled her into my office with one of the four life-size human models, Margaret the Manikin, and gave Kaye a basket of bath and feminine products, demonstrated proper bathing technique, and explained proper use of each hygiene item.

Kaye watched my every movement and heard my every word. She looked wretched and inhibited. I stopped mid-sentence just for clarity.

I was bewildered at her reaction. Why does she not tell me she knows what to do or walk out and slam the door? Is she held captive in this decay?

I resumed the private personal demonstration. Contamination must cease.

Before Kaye left my office, she said, "Thank you. I never knew there was all this stuff. And I even know what to do with it now." She smiled. "Can my mom use some of this?"

"Of course she can."

She hugged me. "Can my mom come see you?"

━═╬═╬═━

Kaye scheduled her mom time at our parent-teacher conference. They had no phone.

Our cafeteria served dinner for parents on conference nights, and Kaye's mom, Roberta, Uncle Bob, and Kaye carried their meals to the lab, where they stayed the entire evening.

Roberta was an older version of Kaye. Plump feet. Fleshy hands. Round body parts with tubular legs. Straw-like hair. Slumped shoulders. Her legs swished when she walked as odor leached. Bacterial? Fungoid? I noticed Roberta holding her right hand in her left, then the left in her right just as Kaye often did.

Uncle Bob had a cocky confidence about him. Worn and filthy. Bald head with a scraggly coarse beard. Rings of grime circled the wrinkles on his bull neck. He stood well over six feet tall and donned a belly-hugging gray-tinged wife-beater, revealing his weathered skin, square shoulders, and well-developed arms. Not bathing must be a family trait carried through the genes.

Uncle Bob told Roberta and Kaye where to sit. Obey. Expressionless.

I talked with Kaye and her mom but Uncle Bob interrupted, speaking for them. I ignored his words and urged him to remain silent. "Please, sir, for a few more minutes. I only have a little more to say."

He made no eye contact with me but blamed me for Kaye's grades and inattention in my boring class. He ravaged us with words and shouted impurities.

"This is a waste of her time, this education crap. And don't be givin' her more female stuff, planting silly ideas in her head to be beautiful. Just look at her. Can't do nothin' with that face."

I stood my ground for Kaye—her ability, her education, her feminism and beauty.

Uncle Bob got in my face but I did not move, though his breath reeked. I stayed put for Kaye and for Roberta—his prisoners.

Uncle Bob strutted to a corner and reached into his pocket, pulling out a cigarette and lighting up.

Determination moved me in his direction. He smelled like a locker room, stale tobacco, and a garbage truck. I felt it seep under my shoes as his eyes cut through me and into my skin until he finally stepped out the back door. Through all this, I kept composure. Four hours. I knew his control infected, causing decay, rot, and gangrene.

Roberta defended Uncle Bob. "Kaye needs to be home. We need her. It's where she belongs."

Does she believe this? Does Kaye believe this? Decay was a slippery slope.

Child Protective Services never got past their lies.

"What did their home smell like? Wouldn't that be neglect or a safety issue?"

Child Protective Services never informed me.

⚒

Roberta and Kaye continued to attend conferences until Kaye graduated six years later. They ate the prepared meals and sat in my lab talking to Betty and me. They told us of life and sorrows.

Uncle Bob never resurfaced in the lab. Kaye never furthered her education. Roberta never found work. Kaye did not know what she wanted. And odors persisted.

Kaye learned she was pregnant. Tears ran down her face. When she refused to name the father, Betty and I shared a knowing glance.

We convinced the two of them to seek shelter and safety and offered our help.

Their dull empty eyes looked at each other and then down, each of them holding her right hand in her left, then her left in her right. An epidemic of fear held them hostage to decay.

AN UNMISTAKABLE SIGN OF
PASSAGE

"You go girl. You can do anything. Nothing will stop you. Wear what you want. Don't worry, be happy."

Two hundred and twenty middle school girls, supervised by four high school girls and ten women, arrived for a planned night of nontraditional career experiences and esteem building. The event was called Girl Power. And there would be no sleep—only food, games, and learning as young girls were fed messages to lift them up. But those well-intended cheers sprouted thin and hollow.

Why did I tell Gloria I would help? I asked myself.

Each girl wore a label depicting her assigned animal group, and each group vocalized with the animal's known sounds. There were unpredictable bears, deceptive peacocks, screeching owls, hair-raising hyenas, agitated skunks, and clapping seals. And the chaperones represented a herd of wandering elephants. The gymnasium sounded like a howling wilderness.

Jean and Lisa volunteered to assist me with teaching the chaperones CPR at the event.

Conversation flowed as we introduced ourselves, but one of the mothers remained quietly outside the circle, her hands folded on her lap.

"For our Girl Power night, I prepared a program I thought would be helpful for you," I began. "A night of learning."

Several minutes into the CPR presentation, Tonya said, "We're not seeing relevance in this CPR. We're a bunch of young mothers whose kids will be teenagers too soon. We need guidance from someone like you who's been through it."

"Yes, I feel like the wandering elephant I was a few minutes ago, all that weight on my shoulders and not knowing where to go," Joyce said as other moms nodded.

I took a deep breath, made a quick mental adjustment, and entertained their wishes.

"Believe me, I question every decision I make," I said, "and every decision my husband makes. Being a mother is the most difficult and most important job we'll ever have. What is weighing on your minds?"

The ladies whispered among themselves and Tonya became their spokeswoman.

"You start," she urged.

At one o'clock in the morning, my words were slow to form. "The first changes I noticed were mood swings and anger, stomping down the hall to their rooms and shutting the doors a bit too loudly."

They smiled, nodded, and said almost in unison, "Yes."

And then an outpouring of personal experiences from all came.

"My daughter does that."

"She's in her room for hours."

"She cries."

"Mine screams."

"Then, after all those antics, she asks us to do something for her."

Then the quiet lady addressed me.

"Please help. I have no idea what to do. My Shannon won't talk to me anymore. We used to go shopping together and have lunch. She'd tell me all about school and friends and her teachers. We giggled, sometimes too loud. Now I get nothing. I'm the dumbest mother on the planet," she said.

Jesse chimed in. "All my Angela wants is to be with her friends. She's on the phone for hours, stays in her room, and watches TV into the wee hours of the morning and then I can't get her up for school. Her grades have dropped from As to barely passing."

"Ladies, I've been right where you are and experienced the same things," I said.

Jean and Lisa, the CPR assistants I had dismissed, joined our circle.

I introduced Lisa as our artist for the evening. She had sketched pictures of each animal and placed them around the school. And beside the elephant sketch stood the outline of a sad-faced little girl not to be seen, a gnome with a wild pixie-like hairdo. Lisa had blocked in a straight bar earring with a bead on each end protruding from the upper left ear. Then she'd added an ear gauge in each earlobe. I wondered if she had sketched herself.

The quiet woman observed Jean's dyed black hair that hung straight about her striking features. She scrutinized her earlobes that drooped like a basset hound's with the gauges but it was the solid black attire, including lipstick and nail polish, at which she gawked.

Jean and Lisa spoke frankly, the mothers remained attentive, and I found an empty chair outside the circle beside the quiet woman.

"Just be cool, no pressure," Lisa said. "Set boundaries and direction, and forgive them. Don't determine what is best for them. They will make mistakes. They will hurt. You can't protect them from everything. Listen with a genuine interest. Encourage good grades and then help them when they're stuck, but don't set the course for their future. Let them be who they are, who they can become."

"Trust your daughters," Jean added. "Hug them. Love them. Share your gifts with them. Share their talents and let 'em know you are proud of them. I was only good enough to look good to the world. I changed that."

"Spend time and show support and respect for what matters to your kids," Lisa continued. "Quit controlling them. Don't judge them or their friends. My friends are important. Sure, my insecurities are always with me, but when someone believes in you, they can be overcome. My parents are swallowed up by ambition and unrealistic expectations. They want me to be a doctor. Dream on. Don't make them write your story; let them write their own. I am going to be a graphic artist."

The quiet woman sat straight in her chair, taking note of Lisa's words. She took a photo out of her purse, rubbed her fingers over it, and closed her eyes. Perhaps she enjoyed a faint shine of identity she once knew.

An exchange of questions and replies continued for the next hour. Alcohol. Dating. Drugs. Anorexia. Bulimia. Parties. Masks came off, and the discussion was brutally honest.

"None of you want your children to suffer or meet heartbreak or tragedy," I said, wrapping up our discussion. "Yet you cannot dead bolt that door. You have to kick it in, face it head-on, and stampede over it, not run into the wilderness. Show up. Your presence alone is the gift your daughters need most. Keep believing. Keep hoping. I am reminded of the twenty-third Psalm and the comfort and hope it gives. And I tell myself that I'm Mom, not God."

All except the quiet woman filed out. Her name was Sharon and she divulged her story that night.

"I lost my oldest daughter, Ashley, to cancer. She was nine at the time. Today she would have turned fifteen. There was nothing any doctor could do to save her. For two years she suffered. I was by her bedside day and night. My husband helped when he could. But we also had Mark and Marissa to take care of, so my mom and mother-in-law helped with them." Sharon struggled with her emotions as she continued. "I sang 'Jesus Loves Me' to Ashley and told her I loved her. It was so dark that night. So late. I closed my eyes and fell asleep. When I awoke, she had passed. I just never knew those words would be the last she ever heard from me. There was so much more to say. I wasn't with her when she needed me."

A tangled mix of tears erupted from us both.

"But Sharon, you were there," I managed. "There is no song more beautiful or any words more needed from a mother."

⋖⊹⊹⋗

Six hours after the sleepless night was over, I met my friend for a late lunch.

Ten minutes passed after the hostess seated me, then twenty. The tables were occupied with a mix of customers. A grumpy gentleman accompanied only by his cell phone sat in the corner. At the table to my right were two women about my age, laughing and talking with their four young children. At the table to my left sat a mother with a messy-haired eleven-year-old daughter wearing torn, grass-stained khakis.

"What did you do today, Bailey?" the girl's mom asked.

Bailey licked her fingers of drips and oozes of ketchup that descended from her french fries. "We played soccer, girls against boys. We won. I made three goals. My knee's skinned up an' my pants have a hole in 'em."

The girl giggled with pride, and her mom put her salad fork down, reached across the table, and clutched her daughter's ketchupy, salt-laden hands.

"You have to be more careful," she said. "I really don't think you should play soccer. Why can't you just join the art or science club? I don't want you hurt. And you've gone and ruined another pair of khakis."

Bailey gave her mom an unfavorable smile and spoke in a pleading voice.

"Geez Mom, I'm fine. We all play like that. And I've decided to try out for the school soccer team. Gotta give me some space and stop checkin' up on me all the time. Quit makin' me be you. I wanna dress like the other kids and wear jeans. And you know I like soccer."

Soon their conversation continued in laughter and smiles.

"Let's have a family night of games," her mom said. "Maybe Ally, your new friend, can come over."

I smiled at the unmistakable sign of passage.

PART SIX

a time to tear, and a time to sew;
a time to keep silence, and a time to speak...

Ecclesiastes 3:7 ESV

BAKED BY ABBY

Our guest speaker, Steve Harriman, a delightful young RN from the local hospital's emergency department, was in the middle of his presentation when Abby leaned toward Nikki.

Abby danced two colorful clothespins decorated with yellow yarn hair, marker dot eyes, raisin noses, and licorice smiles on her desk. Then I noticed the paper skirts. Tampons!

My neck tightened and my veins popped out as my head tilted to the side in anger. Breathing became an effort as the presentation wrapped up with student questions and I directed Abby to my office.

"What were you thinking?" I asked.

She smiled, shrugging it off. "I'm sorry. I...I didn't mean to upset you."

Is she clueless to basic manners? My expression said it all, and Abby apologized to Nurse Harriman and to the class.

I smiled inside as Abby walked over to me and grabbed my hands with a tear in her eye. Perhaps we will benefit from this fiasco, I thought.

The time arrived for students to practice their nurse aide skills: seventy-five hours of training and five days at the local nursing home. I loved these moments. Students applied knowledge, communicated with residents, and learned structured routines and responsibility.

On her meal break Abby shared her small sack lunch of a candy bar, chips, and a soda with Madison. I offered to buy them a sandwich and fruit from the vending machine but both refused.

"I'm used to sharin' my food," Abby said. "I make sure my younger brothers and sisters eat first. Sometimes there's not enough for me 'cause I got to save somethin' for my mom when she gets home from her job."

Poverty reared its ugly head.

Abby was the oldest of five. Her mother worked two jobs to earn a meager wage. Abby loved to create: craft, paint, and write fiction. She taught her sisters various crafts, cleaned the house, did laundry, and packed school lunches when there was food. She cooked, washed dishes, and helped her siblings with their homework. Her schoolwork was an afterthought. Abby baked pies and cookies and even a special filled cake creation when she could buy the jelly and peanut butter. Her mom was seldom home so Abby did what she could for her family. She was well aware of life's harsh realities and necessary sacrifices.

The next evening I ordered pizza for my students. Wednesday I prepared chicken with rice in my crockpot. Thursday we had salad with garlic bread. And Friday I brought soup. And we celebrated a new success each day.

I hesitated for two weeks to phone Abby's mother. Suppose I am wrong? What if Abby is up to creative storytelling about her home life? Teenage girls change stories like they change clothes. But there were five children to consider. And the lack of food dehumanized her family. If I did nothing it would be a blot on my conscience forever. If the students did nothing, it would be a blot on the school. So I phoned midday.

Her mom answered with a quiet pleasantness in her voice, a phantom pain in her words. There was no closet full of clothes, no cupboards full of food, no fancy house. There was emptiness in her heart and despair in her soul. I heard exhaustion from her jobs and love for her children. She was determined to provide and improve life for her children. In spite of this, she insisted her family share what little they had with others in need. I grasped a mother's sorrow yet sensed her strength. And I could only return words of kindness.

A cookie sat on my desk wrapped in a napkin. On top was a scrap of torn notebook paper that read, "Baked by Abby."

Several weeks later I stumbled upon a chance to help the class study about community and contribute to Abby's family. My students began a collection of needs given to me by Abby's mom, Mrs. Hart. The items our class collected seemed ordinary: socks, blankets, sheets, soap, toothpaste, and T-shirts. But these were luxuries for Abby's family, true needs. The local grocer gift card from the school staff seemed inadequate but it was a blessing for the family struggling.

Visions of Abby's life cleared over the weeks. She hungered to employ her own talents and craved her own life's recipe rather than her current hardship path.

I drove to Abby's isolated house to deliver the collected items. Mrs. Hart and Abby welcomed me and Mrs. Hart's eyes welled with tears. The entire family was gracious and offered me their hospitality. I stayed for dinner thinking of my own family.

We sat at a rough-hewn, lopsided table. Abby's sisters were proud of their flower arrangement, dandelions in a milk jug vase. Abby's brother served the meal—macaroni and cheese casserole and a salad of dandelion greens—on the mismatched plates. They shared what they had in humble gratitude. I witnessed Mrs. Hart's unselfish spirit in her children's behavior. This family knew hardship and love. The doors of their hearts were open to all.

As I drove home I realized that what was beautiful to them was peculiar to others. What was normal family use was squalor and laziness to others. What was acceptable to them was laughed at or pitied by others.

As a nurse and an educator, I cycled through happy unhappy moments with others. It was moments like those with Mrs. Hart and her family that made the world come alive. I forgot the dimness that loomed and saw hope behind doors. Mrs. Hart had the key.

UNTOLD WOUNDS

L ate one evening after school, I saw so much more work ahead of me. With only the custodians in the building I knew there'd be no interruptions. I heard my classroom door open and saw Reagan awaiting my response.

It had been about five years since I'd heard from her, and she wanted to talk.

Reagan grew up in a world of silence and untold wounds.

"When I was four it was such fun playing in the yard with my friends. My mom made fruit punch even though she was busy with her legal work. The older kids would sneak next door to the neighbor lady's garden and eat her strawberries while I hid in the hedge and watched," Reagan began. "One day that grizzly old neighbor lady ran out on her porch, screaming and shaking her fist at the kids. And then she stared straight at me and pointed her finger. I peed my pants and ran home to Mom in tears. Several weeks later a couple of the older boys said I could go with them to eat strawberries and they'd protect me from the neighbor lady, so I went.

The neighbor never saw us that day. I felt safe with them. They were like the brothers I didn't have."

Her eyes welled with tears, and her words stopped. She placed her trembling hands on my desk, the right over the left, and I covered them with mine.

"I'm okay. Please, I need to tell you. I must. Just give me a minute."

Reagan, with her square face and almond-shaped eyes, wriggled in her chair and took a deep breath.

"We went into the woods on our favorite path. Then one of them pulled me into the weeds. While one held me down, the other...well...they took turns. After they finished they left me all alone in the weeds with dying flowers." She cried seemingly unending tears. "Sometimes I wonder how I got up each morning or how I even smiled. I decided in seventh grade to lose myself in school work and books. I buried my emotions in a great, deep hole to forget all about what happened. But my pain would not go away. I fought it, but it erupted, mostly at home. Our family was a loving one, so Mom and Dad thought my outbursts were just growing teenage stuff. I never told them about that awful day 'cause everybody liked those boys. But I knew what they were really like." Reagan gasped for air as though underwater with no way out. "Anyway, like I was saying, life was pointless. I was nasty to everybody—manipulative and causing trouble. I'm so sorry for that and sorry I treated you the way I did. You were always happy and nice to me and my classmates and so determined to help us learn that I hated you for it. I laughed at you, mocked you, and made snide remarks in class."

"I know and—" I started, but Reagan interrupted, compelled to vomit up the remainder of her story.

"I worked at causing trouble in class. I wanted you to hate me. But I knew you never did. I refused to talk with you or let you help me. I was smart enough without you. My hatred got deeper and deeper. I went off to college pretending everything was okay. I thought I had become good at wearing masks. After three semesters I dropped out to work the streets. I stopped eating and let alcohol fill my needs."

I sat in silence and listened.

"One night a priest walked by and saw me cowering in the corner of a building on a street corner. My face was bruised and swollen. I tasted my own blood and I hurt. I was shivering from cold and hunger and crying that I was still alive. The priest stopped and talked to me, then helped me to a shelter. That priest came every day to visit me. I hated him. He was persistent like you. After several weeks I had him call my parents. From then on Mom and Dad have done so much to help me. Mom quit her law office and works part-time consulting. Dad runs his company from home. I knew they loved me, but I still didn't heal quickly after I told them what happened to me as a child. I went through rehab and four counselors, but the counselor I have now is great. All those years I felt stained and ruined. What I had done was so bad and I was so ashamed that I couldn't tell anyone. My counselor said those boys stole my childhood. Anyway, I just had to tell you what happened to me and let you know that I am so, so sorry about how I treated you."

I placed my hands over hers and said, "I'm just glad you're getting help now and moving on with your life."

Reagan wiped her eyes and almost smiled.

"I am back in college working on a business degree. Oh, and I have to tell you, I work in a flower shop. Can you believe that? I hated flowers for the longest time. And I hated you for having us plant those crazy pots with flowers for the elderly and handicapped. I hated the flowers you'd put on your desk."

"Yes, I remember," I said. "One day I watched three pots fall to the floor from your hands in what you called *accidents*. And I remember you knocked over the vase of daisies on my desk also. I knew something was bothering you but you weren't ready to share yet."

On my way home red geraniums huddled in doorways and on front stoops and marigolds lined walkways. Gardens flourished with bushes and azaleas, radiating a sweet floral tang. There were grasses and weeds and wildflowers and the loveliest wild daisies, all beauty in pursuit of survival.

LOTUS TEA

"Vietnam is a Southeast Asian country on the South China Sea. It's known for its beaches, rivers, Buddhist pagodas, and bustling cities. Hanoi, the capital, pays homage to the nation's iconic communist-era leader, Ho Chi Minh, with a huge marble mausoleum. The city was once known as Saigon. It has French landmarks plus Vietnamese war history museums and the Cu Chi tunnels used by Viet Cong soldiers during the Vietnam War."

Violet spoke with confidence and authority.

"I chose to do my culture-in-health care report on Vietnam because I am the daughter of a Vietnamese woman. Yet I never knew her. My father is an American who served as a Marine during the Vietnam War. He was one of the last to leave the country. Dad was helping evacuate refugees. My mother lived on the streets of Saigon. She was not able to leave the country. I was born in an alley. Before my mother died, she put me on the doorstep of some mission. Several years later Dad received a letter and learned he had a daughter. Although he wasn't sure if the letter was bogus or not, he came for me. The orphanage where I lived believed that I was about three-years-old then, but no one really knows my age. Since I had unhealthy milk and scraps of nourishment during those years, my bones and body didn't grow as it should have."

The class waited for more. I closed my eyes. In darkness I felt the damp, smelled human waste and rotting vegetation, and heard the cries of starving babies and wails of mothers.

Violet continued. "The health care was poor then, but improvements have been made in availability of equipment and hospitals. The poor treat themselves. The people are plagued with mosquitoes. They carry disease: malaria, dengue fever, and encephalitis. Vaccines...they come to America for a better life...fundamental foods include rice, soup, spring rolls, and..."

Violet finished her report and gave samples of pho and bánh cuốn, soup and rice crepes, seasoned in a mixture of spices: lemongrass, cilantro, curry. We drank lotus tea.

A week later I learned that Violet's dad, Mr. Mitchell, spoke to the social studies classes regarding the war. He limped to my lab with his cane. His hair was long and wiry and a bushy beard hid his face. He scanned the room, checking our equipment as though it may attack him.

"Thank you for teaching and helping Violet. She's not had it easy," he said.

But before I could speak, he dismissed me and did an about-face.

"Sir, would you like to sit?" I called after him. "I can offer you coffee. We could talk."

But Mr. Mitchell continued out the door.

⤛⊦⊹⤜

Violet careened and staggered, then lurched forward and I broke her fall.

She broadcasted across the lab, "I'm tired of this constant humiliation, trying to act normal when I'm not. I'm tired of doctors, my dad, and my mom. I hate myself, my life."

"Is there something you would like to talk about?" I asked when I got to her to my office.

Violet looked at me, tears on the threshold of flowing. She opened her mouth but words did not come. I handed her a tissue and stepped out of the office, promising to be back in a few minutes. She nodded and tried not to look at me shamefaced.

I returned in fifteen minutes and she looked me in the eye.

"I do want to talk," she sighed. "When I was born my bones were deformed. I have food here and have grown over the past ten years. After eight years of seeing doctors and searching for help, my parents can no longer afford it. I've had surgeries on my clubbed feet, webbed toes, and several muscles and tendons. I've been poked and prodded. I've had splints and casts. Nothing really was very successful. I do all kinds of exercises to get better."

"Do you think you're better?"

"Well, you can see I'm still crooked. I falter and stumble when I walk. Kids make fun of me, tease me, and laugh. You know how it is. Your class helps us understand other people and accept each other as we are. I like that. I'll never be better. I guess I just don't want to cause more embarrassment for my parents. I want to be like everyone else."

I prayed for her battle not to worsen, that she would have the strength to survive, and that she could resist the despair.

⊱✦⊰

Autumn staggered into winter and it was time to learn the proper procedure when performing an electrocardiogram (EKG).

I'd done EKGs before, but the equipment had been different— less technologically advanced. I reviewed all directions from the manual after school the day prior to the lab, but it seemed to be in a foreign language I had never learned.

Violet returned to school that afternoon for her English note-book, and, aware of my frustration with technology, took the directions and input the necessary data into the machine. We then hooked electrodes to Kenny, a custodian and our patient, and Violet went through the entire procedure and then taught me.

"I'd love to work in the computer world," she said. "Mom says no. Dad doesn't care. They're divorced, you know."

"No. I didn't know," I said, planning in my head to improvise instruction for her in an ancillary service.

The next day Violet was my lab assistant, supporting the students as they performed the required skills.

By spring, Violet had begun sharing more of her days with me.

"Mom's getting married in June," she told me. "Since the divorce I have lived with my dad. Mom wants nothing to do with me anymore. Dad's started using porn sites. He's always on the internet. Makes me watch sometimes. Says I can learn things."

I inhaled with my mouth open. This man who fathered Violet, who took her from a world of stress and strife to give her a new country?

She continued. "It's awful. I tell him I don't want to look. He doesn't care. I guess he doesn't care about anything anymore."

⟩+⟨

Worry came that my meeting with Violet's mom, Ann, would be a tragedy and that I might wound more than I would help.

We met at a city park and sat on a bench by the duck pond.

I began, "Has Violet talked with you lately?"

She shrugged and crinkled her nose. "Why should she?"

"Well, I just thought she would. She's quite unhappy with her father. You know—"

Ann interrupted in rapid fire. "He immerses himself in porn and she's worried. Violet's a tough girl. She'll survive. I mean, she's not even my daughter. Never did want her. I still have no idea why Mitch had to go back over there and find her. And that couldn't be the end of it. He had to bring her back here."

"Violet had a troubled childhood—"

Again, I was interrupted.

"So she struggles. What about her dad and me? We gave up a lot of things for her and I'm tired of it. It was time I leave them both to their own ruin."

"She makes every effort to be loved," I said. "You are her mother. You are all she's known. She loves you, needs you, and wants to be with you."

The next morning I braved the cold administration office to report Violet's exposure to pornography.

The following week, Violet informed me, "Dad was furious when I got home last Friday. Child Protective Services visited him about his porn. He gave them a different computer and they fell for it. He's clever with all that stuff. But he said when I graduate this spring, I'm to move out. Oh, where will I go? What will I do 'cause Mom sure doesn't want me around?"

I informed our guidance department and they searched for places for her to live and found scholarships she could apply for. The local women's shelter let Violet live in one of their small rooms.

⚔︎

Two years later I saw Violet at the local college campus. With her was a stack of books and a thermos of lotus tea.

"I floundered my first year here. Then I had to decide a major. You helped with all the medical office stuff you had me input into the computer. Yet I felt like I was just throwing things up in the air, hoping something would land and look promising. A medical records career has landed. I figure over time, after I earn my college degree and get a job, I'll know my exact direction and what steps to take up the career ladder."

"I'm really glad to hear that. I see you still drink your lotus tea."

"Yes, I do. I think I always will. After all it's a part of me, my heritage—the part I know so little about."

"And what is happening with your parents?"

"I never see them. Dad did give in and pays tuition. I text a thank you every time he sends the money. Still does his porn and never did get caught. Mom moved away. I work at Dr. Stark's pediatric office inputting patient data. They're all my family now."

We locked eyes, smiled, and finished our lotus tea.

DESSERT HAWK

Every Friday the West Park Baptist Church's soup kitchen offered the Lord's word, prayer, warmth, and food. About two hundred tattered men, women, and children flowed into the sanctuary to listen to the pastor's required service before eating dinner.

The attendees were broken, dirty, hungry, and desperate people. Some were mothers, fathers, gang members, or alcoholics. Some held jobs and some fought for our country. Some were ill, handicapped, or psychotic. They smelled of vomit, body excrement, and alcohol. They carried trash and paper bags, wore oversize coats and pants, and were lucky to carry an old purse or drag a suitcase. They collected newspapers and cardboard. There was nothing to cheer or sing about. Some mumbled to themselves or whoever listened but internally they screamed.

That night my class made all the desserts and five of us, including Holly, stayed to help serve. The students displayed an array of sweets: triple-layer chocolate cake, a Texas sheet cake, no-bake cookies, melt-in-your mouth fudge, orange puffs, and cherry almond sugar cookies. Also on the table were a pumpkin pie, two apple pies, a blueberry cobbler, and four dozen donuts.

The pastor's rule was one helping until all had been served but our guests craved more than one dessert. Goldie tottered to our table and asked for another piece of triple-layer chocolate cake. I saw no harm and snuck her a piece. Then Dessert Hawk swooped in and chided me. Holly giggled and couldn't wait to tell her classmates.

Throughout the evening Holly and I chit-chatted over the dessert table. At first our conversation was run-of-the-mill, then it changed abruptly.

"I've always been a quiet kid, so when I felt like being quieter no one gave me a thought. I sleep about four hours each night, and now I don't eat much. I've lost forty pounds in a few months. No one sees me," Holly confided.

"Holly, what do you think the problem is?"

"Oh, who knows?" She hung her head. "Ya know...um...I'm hardly worth much. So why should I care about anything like school, friends, family? I'm just a burden to them, a bother."

"Do you think that pushes them further away?" I asked.

"I'm just sick of school, of everything. Um...I know what you'll say...that I have a family, food, and parents who love me. But I'm really a mess, mixed up, I guess. No one understands me."

⤙⤚

Monday morning the phone rang. It was Holly.

"My grandmother died last night—you know, the one we live beside. She had a stroke. We rushed her to the hospital, then she was taken by helicopter to University Hospital. They did CPR. I'll miss her. I won't be in lab today. I might miss the whole week."

No tears. Bland.

I asked, "Were you close with your grandmother?"

"Grandma lived next door to us. She raised me from birth," she said, emotionless with laughter in the background.

Holly detailed, step-by-step, all procedures done on her grandmother from the moment she was admitted to the ICU unit until she died. But her words were hollow and robotic.

Cold-heartedness for a loved one's death concerned me, and all morning those robotic words haunted me. Holly had mirrored my lecture notes on patient care in ICU and death. At least she knew the lessons, except for grief, I thought.

I walked a tightrope and called Holly's parents.

Three days later Holly's mom, Mrs. Sherrin, returned my call.

My sympathies were met with dead silence over the phone.

"What do you mean, my mother's death?" Mrs. Sherrin asked.

I explained my conversation with Holly. More silence followed by icy numbness.

The next morning Holly followed her mother into the lab with shoulders drooping and head lowered. Holly sat and looked at the floor while Mrs. Sherrin and I went to my office.

Mrs. Sherrin said, "I've always been there for her, even when I acted like I wasn't. I was there when she fell and for her second-grade play. I was there when she sang her first solo in choir and when she had her first dance recital and her first formal. I read to her, praised her, taught her manners. We laughed together, played Candyland®, and made Christmas ornaments."

I nodded.

"There were pizza parties and sleepovers. I hugged her, kissed her, and squeezed her because no one knows how long the ones we love stay. I now fear that the Holly I knew has left me. It happened slowly and before I realized it. She became someone I don't know. But I love her. I always will."

"Have you noticed any changes in her over the last few years or months?" I asked.

"I have, now that you mention it. She's not eating right."

It's easy to miss the obvious signs in those around you.

"Do you think something else is going on with her?" I asked.

"I'd imagine it's teenage hormones."

"Mrs. Sherrin, do you think maybe Holly is depressed? Maybe has been for some time?"

Dark smudged lines marked her face.

"Oh no...what will...I can't talk with anyone about this—not family, not friends. Holly listens to you. Please help her understand I love her."

I shifted in my chair giving me some time to gather words. "I think Holly needs much more help than I can give her. She needs a professionally trained counselor or psychologist. Holly considers herself worthless and her deceit about her grandmother shows a lack of remorse. And another thing, I don't think too much time alone is healthy for Holly right now."

Mrs. Sherrin listened intently as tears flowed until the smudge lines on her face ran together.

"We will get her the best help we can afford. My husband and I have not given her the attention she needs but we do love her."

⇥⇤

For the fifth week Holly and I guarded the dessert table. We were pros at warding off customers with two dessert requests. Both of us had a watchful eye for Dessert Hawk. That night, though, Dessert Hawk sat in a corner, watchful of society's throwaway lineup as it passed through the doorway. She waited while workers cleaned tables, did dishes, stacked chairs, and scrubbed floors. Concerned, I dried my sudsy hands and walked over to talk with her. Holly tagged along.

"A year ago I was homeless and living behind an old coffee shop, my daughter and I," Dessert Hawk told us. "We watched people come and go with their fancy coffee and breakfast to fill their bellies. None for us. One day I told myself we would get through this and I did. But drugs and street promises barred her from leaving. Haven't seen her for five years this very day. I love her and always will. So I wait for her, here."

Holly grabbed her hand, and gradually, tears formed. I returned to the dirty dishes. Holly and Dessert Hawk conversed for two more hours as the pastor and I sat outside on the church steps waiting.

Two women—one young, one older—in search of a second chance, a dream.

PADLOCK

As I made rounds Blake slept under one of the beds. He jolted and bumped his head on the underside of the bed frame when he was caught.

"You will finish this assignment today, young man. Where is Jason?" I asked.

Jason appeared at once from somewhere behind me.

An hour later I heard commotion and the students huddled in Jason and Blake's corner. And I wondered what it was this time.

Jason sat in a wheelchair while Blake lounged in the Geri chair. They're dressed in patient gowns, paper slippers, and ratty gray wigs. Jason hugged a purse and Blake cuddled a stuffed bear and dragged a cane. They rolled forward, propelled by their legs, circling the room. They did a simultaneous roll, symbiotic, with the two chairs held together by a hospital sheet. They chattered at each other, their classmates, and me with shaky voices that sounded like rusty hinges.

"I ain't dead yet. Did no one tell you I'm slow? You're getting old. Watch where you're goin' in that wheelchair. Dang it, I got to fart. Out of my way. I need my dentures."

"Gather yourself, get back to work, and stop carrying on like this," I demanded, fighting laughter as the class broke into guffaws.

After school was out, an upset Mr. Parks visited my lab.

"Did you know Jason and Blake are skipping my class?" he asked. "Every day for the last seven days I've called home and sent letters to their parents. The last day I saw them, they stood up during class and threw spicy candy across the room to their class-mates. You know, those red-hot mouth-scorching balls that are big enough to break a person's jaw. All those two ever do is disrupt class. They think they are clever and said it related to chemistry, atomic and all. I was furious."

"I had no idea," I said. "I will talk with them tomorrow. They need to be disciplined and I, too, will reach out to the parents and have them contact you."

<hr />

A fire extinguisher spraying is an intriguing sight, especially when unmanned and spewing chemicals throughout the air in a classroom.

I ordered my students, "Leave the room now."

There was no fire, yet chemicals bathed the room in a white powder. Oxygen would soon be depleted and my skin burned cold while my class stood outside in the hallway, choking and coughing. It was an ugly sight so I hustled them to the library.

I planned to return to the lab to stop the extinguisher's snaking across the floor but I saw a mass of administrators in stride and in the middle, the superintendent.

My heart pounded and my hands trembled in panic. I fell in step with the front line and tried to explain.

"Jason and Blake were doing a routine check of fire extinguish-ers," I began. "Jason dropped ours and the little key dislodged from the squeeze bar and the nozzle stuck, causing this mess."

I wasn't sure I believed my own words. Maybe I should padlock the squeeze bar.

"Mess!" boomed the superintendent. My heart galloped as his dominance was made known. "Are you aware of the damage Jason caused? The chaos Blake sparked? Do you know all the outside agencies involved?"

While he briefed me on procedure, I heard the extinguisher empty and I timidly said, "I am truly sorry for this debacle."

With a flaming retort, he said, "Yes, and you should be. Now send those two responsible to my office at once. I will deal with you after school."

The administrative mass about-faced and only the custodian stayed behind to clean the lab.

From the dental lab I borrowed goggles, a mask, gloves, and an oversize white biohazard outfit to protect my skin so I could assist Mac. We looked like giant marshmallows.

Jason and Blake faced a ten-day suspension since it was their second offense for destruction of school property. I sustained rebuke with severe words of reprimand from not only the superintendent but also the displeased fire marshal.

⋙⟶⟵⋘

When Blake and Jason returned, their antics continued.

We studied genetics for a few days and Jason inquired, "Do twins know that one of them is unplanned?"

The class laughed.

During a practice session for proper phlebotomy procedure, I caught Jason and Blake playing rock, paper, scissors.

Jason said, "Did you know losing a game is just as hard as trying to win?"

"Enough. To my office, both of you," I called.

Words of a past college instructor replayed in my head: "Never laugh or smile so no patient thinks you treat their situation without proper weight. Be nothing less than professional."

That should accomplish the same with students. I must stop the shenanigans.

For three weeks the jokes decreased. But these two only encouraged and fed off of one another. The hilarity of their antics coated the room with laughter. They spoofed diseases, medical terminology, and skills. Jason acted out the definitions and needed clarifications. Blake provided one-liners and monologues. They created a list of their spoofs and stood at the door, passing them out as the students entered.

I read a few. "Caesarian Section is a neighborhood in Rome. Bacteria is the back door to our cafeteria. Pyro is the line of pies at the bakery. Urine is opposite of you're out. Intubate is a fisherman's urge. Enema is not my friend."

Absurd. I stopped reading with a hidden smile regarding these two complex young men.

One morning they stood in front of the class at the lectern impersonating me. Both wore wigs and, of course, the class laughed. I stepped back and listened as Jason retaught my classroom rules and expectations. I laughed with the class as he imitated my behaviors, speech, and walk. Blake reviewed health and safety mandates. He leaned over the podium and scanned the room, an imitation of my announcement to begin class. His one-liners voiced the illogical. And despite the ridiculousness, students engaged as they dialogued a review for the upcoming test.

These two lived to be my nemeses. They were hopeless incorrigibles their junior year, both acting out inappropriately with their amazing sense of humor. They derailed my lesson plans and stole the spotlight. Yet I saw creativity develop.

I made every effort to keep focus and classroom management. I changed my way of thinking and saw them differently than many of my colleagues. What if they were gifted, not simply jerks who craved attention? What if they were misguided, not troublemakers?

By their senior year, I wondered if they were bored, confused, or attention grabbing. Perhaps they were hiding behind the humor.

All they shared with me was this: "We like to laugh and enjoy life. Why should we sweat the trivial stuff or even life itself? Gotta laugh, ya know."

No matter, they made the class and me laugh and helped the students study. I encouraged their strengths, so Blake and Jason could bring the class to life.

Humor, a redemptive power, brightened the work and shrunk the stress and tension. Humor enhanced learning and heightened retention. Humor is a form of wisdom, a quality I wanted in my classroom and in my life.

Several years later they returned to lab. Blake had become a respiratory therapist and Jason a Navy lieutenant.

WORDS NOT SPOKEN

Trevor held Aleshia's legs so she wouldn't fall as she crawled out the lab window onto the sidewalk.

I waved to stop her and squawked, "Freeze right there. And get back in this room."

Ignored, my words flew out the window and I stormed over.

"Save the bird," the class cheered.

"What bird?" I asked.

Trevor said, "A female cardinal flew into the window. We're saving her. See, she's lying out there on the grass."

I looked as he pointed. She had injured her wing. A male cardinal perched on the fence that shadowed the pavement, his metallic chirp warning his mate of intruders.

Garrett handed Aleshia a small container of water for the birds and Sophia passed her a petri dish of sunflower seeds. Then Aleshia tried to climb back in through the window.

In a firm yet out-of-control voice, I squawked again, "Stop right there and walk around to the back hallway door."

That door was camera-monitored like the sidewalk and kept locked for safety.

"Trevor, please open the door for Aleshia," I said.

The students returned to their desks, awaiting the test, as I told Aleshia and Trevor that I intended to contact their parents, who worked at the school.

As school ended the supervisor, Mr. Stinson, visited me. He had seen the entire cardinal escapade. I wanted to become invisible.

He admonished my classroom management and criticized my discipline.

"Just where were you when they were crawling out windows, playing with birds?" he asked.

"I was with students at the other end of the lab," I replied, attempting to defend myself.

"Where are your safety rules and your discipline plan? You can bet I'll be reviewing them and there will be some changes."

"Yes, sir. But these are two kind and loving students, top in their class," I said. "They're both intelligent and on their way to college. You know what they were doing? Trying to save a bird's life. They even gave her a name: Tiki. I agree that they went about it all wrong and I, too, made errors. I'm very sorry. The students and I will work this out. After all aren't I here to guide them?"

He sighed.

"With time they'll realize their errors. It's a respect they deserve. Won't it be better if they come to your office to apologize for their behavior?" I added.

He didn't answer. I handed him a copy of my management strategy and he left.

Minutes later Austin appeared in my office wanting to take the test.

"Austin, you were absent," I said. "I'll have to create a make-up test that you can take Monday or Tuesday."

"Please, please. I studied so hard for this test," he begged.

"Austin, school is over for the day. You know the rules."

His shoulders drooped and his head sagged as he turned away. "What is it, Austin?"

He collapsed like a broken bird crumbling to the ground. His face became bright red as his eyes moistened with tears.

"It's Mr. Scott from my home school. He hates me 'cause of my brother. I was running to the bus to get me here and I didn't make it, so he asked me how I'd get to school. I told him I had no way to get here and he hauled me to the office for skipping school." His agitation spread. "I got mad and cursed him. My bad. I ran out when Mr. Scott started talking about my brother. I hate that place and Mr. Scott. I got suspended for five days an' it starts Monday. My mom brought me here and she's out doin' her shopping while I take the test. Please."

I waited twenty minutes while he paced back and forth in the lab, punching the tables as he walked, and then I gave him his test.

Thirty minutes later, his mother, Mrs. Ridgeway, arrived.

"Ryan was a bad seed, like his dad," she said. "See, my husband was a drunk but he's dead now, from drinkin' so much. Ryan stole a car at age thirteen and robbed our neighbor's house when he was fifteen. I had him in counseling, but it didn't help much. He started to skip school and got into drugs and drinkin'. That's when his grades dropped."

"I didn't know that, Mrs. Ridgeway," I said.

"No, you wouldn't, but Mr. Scott did and that's my fault. Ryan wanted to play football, so I went to Mr. Scott and told him about Ryan and how that just might help him. At first it was the best thing ever. Ryan worked hard to get his grades back up and he was even playin' in the junior varsity games."

"That sounds great. You must've been proud."

"I was, but it didn't last long 'cause that scumbag, Scott, made fun of some of the kids. They hadn't physically grown up enough for him, if ya get my point. He pointed it all out in the locker room.

Ryan defended those kids an' got in Scott's face. Then that son of a gun started in on Ryan. He had the gall to mock his father—told Ryan he was a no-good loser just like his dad. Ryan doubled his fists, but Scott held him down."

Ryan stood up for his father as any son would. His teammates never knew why he defended them. Ryan knew what it was like to be scorned, to be the underdog. He left home. His mom worked long hours at the local ice cream shop and Austin worked evenings at the local pizza shop. Ryan appeared nowhere.

"Perhaps we should focus on Austin's problems," I suggested.

"That scumbag, Scott, is gonna destroy Austin just like he did Ryan with his demeaning and humiliating comments. And you are prob'ly no better. I know Austin adores you, but you're part of the system. Suspended at his home school and it carries over here. No one'll help him."

"I'll do what I can, Mrs. Ridgeway," I promised.

Silence filled the room with a shattered life and so many unsaid words about this family's heartbreak, words Austin had never shared. Austin wiped his tear-filled eyes on his uniform sleeve.

Austin had direction. He wanted to go into occupational therapy and work with children.

"You'll have to keep your grades up and persevere," I told him. "Have you considered starting the first two years of school at our community college? I'll do what I can to help you with scholarships, loans, and grants."

"I've considered that. It'd be cheaper for my mom," he said.

I knew Austin had lofty and noble goals. He wanted to fly high unrestrained and reach his potential, no matter what challenges he might face. But had that day been too much for him to accept and survive? Had he landed a bit too hard like Tiki? Or had it equipped him for tomorrow?

⇥⊹⊹⇤

The metallic chirp of a cardinal twittered in the air. I walked down the path toward our cardinals and kneeled next to Tiki.

The water and sunflower seeds remained at her side. I wanted to touch Tiki and replace her feathers—that part of her that she had lost. Her beak opened and I heard a wheeze. Tiki's tail bobbed up and down with each little breath. I felt a chill as her eyes grew dim. Tiki surrendered life since we were unable to protect and rescue her.

PART SEVEN

a time to love, and a time to hate;
a time for war, and a time for peace.

Ecclesiastes 3:8 ESV

THE MISSING KEY

Monday morning I reported to Supervisor Turner's office. Child Protective Services case worker, Mrs. Hampton, told us that Marcia had run away over the weekend.

Mrs. Hampton read from her notes the details as told to her by Marcia's foster sister: "She dressed in all her clothes: several T-shirts, a sweater, a pair of pajamas, her Cavalier sweatshirt, and a pair of jeans. After the family went to bed, she slipped out the front door and took her backpack and everything she owned—you know, toothbrush, toothpaste, nail polish, mascara, hairbrush, and whatever else. She found her medicine and took a bunch of papers. Don't know why she'd care. Just before walking away, she snatched her skateboard and guitar case from the garage. She left a bunch of books."

Marcia, her name was Marcia. But Mrs. Hampton never called her by her name. Mrs. Hampton's words blurred as I saw large chunks of Marcia's childhood, a time that should've been filled with innocence and joy.

Marcia and her two younger siblings watched their parents drink and scuffle. When their father was not beating their mother, he turned to Marcia and her younger sister, leaving her brother to watch how it was done. They saw their mother try to shoot their father while he held another gun to Marcia's head. There were frequent visits from the police and numerous hospital trips.

By the time Marcia was eight, the family was beyond repair. The children were sent to foster care and the parents to prison or mental institutions. Rehab failed.

Marcia's focus on school diminished along with her behavior. She lay awake at night, threw tantrums, banged her head against the wall, and locked herself in the bathroom, crying for her brother and sister. By age twelve she was smoking heavily and binge drinking with teenagers. After several disturbances with the law, an affluent cousin of her mother's obtained guardianship of Marcia and her sister. It was there that Marcia expanded her love of music.

The family bought her an acoustic guitar. Hiding in her room for hours, she would listen to the radio while strumming along or fingerpicking her own songs. There were no guns, cigarettes, or booze. But the cousin's husband, Dennis, was a problem. He mistreated and molested the girls. Marcia attempted suicide at fifteen and was removed from the home and placed again in the foster system.

The dilapidated guitar case held Marcia's prized possession. My class had heard her sing and play a song she had written. And one of Marcia's friends told me that Marcia played guitar in her church's band.

Mrs. Hampton jarred me from my thoughts and handed me a card.

"She left this for you," she said.

I laid the folded note on my lap, took a deep breath, and returned to a more recent chunk in Marcia's life.

Her red braids danced and her head bounced as she moved through the lab. Behavior and classwork improved during the year. Instructors spotted potential, but Marcia's goals had vanished a few weeks ago when she veered off course with reckless abandon in a vile outburst. From the hallway, Supervisor Turner had heard the loud rants in my classroom and had taken her to his office. I requested he let me deal with her but with Marcia's defiance and contempt, she was not unnerved or thrown into sorrow and remorse.

In two hours Marcia returned to the lab, her eyebrows narrowed as though to hide the anger behind her eyes. She gathered her books and classwork, then left for lunch.

"I'm only here because the state has power to keep me here," she said as she walked out. "I'm a prisoner in their world. I hate this place. It's like all the others, nothing but dream crushers."

Perhaps that was the moment she decided her world would change again and she would move on. Reality washed over me like a bucket of ice water. It could be I never identified with Marcia's bitterness, her hostile start in life, or how she felt chained to a hated life. Maybe, just maybe, I missed key elements to the severity of her damaged relationships or the passion for her dreams and goals.

I left Supervisor Turner's office with my note, thoughts, and memories. Without the bouncing red-haired braids, my class was tranquil, but it was the beginning of an unpleasant day for Marcia as she drifted into life's unknowns.

Finally, the day ended and I read my note.

Doc,

I just want to tell you how much I appreciate you and everything you've done for me. You're a great teacher with a big heart. You put up with a lot of crap from me, more than you deserved. Just remember your class loves you.

I love how emotional you get when teaching and how passionate you are about nursing or any medical career. I think you're wonderful. I wish I could stay but I can't stand people treating me like a child. Funny, you never did. You really understood me and helped me with my school-work. But, best of all, you let me play my guitar.

It's time to move on from these foster parents. They're all the same, they want the money but not me and my problems. An' they won't help me. I'm leaving to find my dream. It's out there somewhere.

Bye and don't forget me,
Marcia

I smiled and my eyes filled with tears as I read, recalling how beautifully she strummed and sang. No, Marcia, I will not forget you, I thought as I placed her note in my treasure chest.

TIME

I picked up the next letter and the next, working my way through the old tan leather-covered nautical-looking chest that had been my mother's. She had given it to me six months before she passed away. There was a section of lace, embraced with pearls, rolled tightly about her book of poems along with personal notes from her favorite teacher. Cherished words. I used it to hold photos of and letters from my students. Each year I added and revisited the previous, cherishing each pearl.

My eyes focused on a letter from Cody. He wrote from a neighboring state's federal prison seven hundred miles away.

"Hope you remember me, Cody...came late for class every day...I told you why I was always late. We lived in the boondocks...I had to get my two sisters up and to different schools...you never sent me to the office."

How well I remembered Cody. His dark features, tall stature, and confident walk gave the girls pause.

His letter went on: "I think this'll cause you pain, but please know that I always appreciated what you did for me...got angry with you a couple times…most of the time…you gave me hope and a belief in myself…goals…I just got lost in time somewhere."

I felt his pain each time I read his letter.

"…went to some college, then dropped out…worked at a strip club…bouncer…ran with a bad crowd and jumped into some heavy drinking. Along with that came the drugs, women, men, and wild parties."

He enclosed a news article and asked that I read it. It was difficult to accept his crime, hard to believe. He had such potential.

There had been a six-month investigation and it was a neighbor's complaint that eventually led to a search warrant for the residence, where heroin, meth, and cocaine, in addition to illegal arms, were recovered. The meth lab had been in full production. The owner and operator, Cody.

A few weeks later I researched newspaper archives and found a commentary on his trial. Cody had accepted a plea deal with a sentence of fifteen to twenty years in federal prison.

I was still in shock. Skilled, clever, and intelligent with a knack for creativity Cody? He reveled in history and government. His English had not been without flaws, but he had worked diligently to correct them. Cody would be close to twenty-three-years-old now.

Words from his letter echoed in my head: "I hid my feelings and behavior for years, until they were bigger than I was—the hatred, bitterness, and anger."

I never remember him as angry or full of hatred. He was jovial and always had a good word for everyone. He kept the gossipers in the class quiet and muted the drama queens.

"Finally I took responsibility for what I did…I read a lot…the Bible… studying English now…but it's hard…make good choices next time…time is priceless, a gift…I wasted it…time I will never get back."

In his fortress, time ticks slowly by with no rhythm. One day, though, he'll be set free from that time and space.

"Thank you for all you did for me. And show Mr. Ferguson this note. He's still teaching chemistry, right? When I get out of here, I'll come see you. Maybe we could get coffee and talk."

⟞⟨⊢ ⊣⟩⟝

Years later I stepped out of the van and along with the sound of crunching gravel I heard the unrestrained hammering of my heart. Cody was already there, sitting at a small table in the coffee shop.

His enormous hands had calluses and battle scars from burns. His nails were bitten and rough and the absent-minded knuckle cracking sounded louder as he told each prison story. It was an uncomfortable conversation.

We sat and talked for several hours. Cody was different—thinner with a shaved head. And eyes that used to dance with life were dim. But it was the scarring of the soul that was the hardest to swallow.

With his prison sentence complete, the season of shifting into a new, unknown role was upon him. He was working at a fast-food chain and studying restaurant management at the local college.

THE FOLDED NOTE

It was a sleepy Monday near the end of the school year when Trista handed me a page of notebook paper folded into sixteen equal sections. I unfolded it to find a note addressed to me—a one-page, four-section message divided into four quadrants. The writing was so tiny I had to pull out my magnifying glass. The note was jumbled and contained misspelled words, which I attributed to Trista's learning and developmental growth.

Sorry I didn't get my work done. I had to spend the whole weekend taking care of Grampa. He had a heart attack two months ago. Doc says his heart, lungs, and kidneys aren't working very well. He's got hepititis C too. My grandma had surgery about a year ago to take out cancer under her left breast and armpit. They figured out the cancer's now in her bones. She can walk and stuff, just gets so weak, you know. So I was there all weekend cooking, cleaning, taking out the trash, and helping them bathe. Some days I feel like I'm the trash.

There's a home health nurse but she can't stay all the time and that's sad. That's why I live with them. There's no car. I ride the bus everywhere. I know this ain't good for my grade. I take all blame. I have went and been tested for hepititis. The tests come back negitive. Me and my aunt wiped the toilet with bleach before each use and used a lot of hand sanitizer and handwashing, disinfecting and sterilizating like you taught us for home care. We use antimicrobial soap too and wash our hands a lot. Lucky for us it works. My grandma was tested for hepititis C. Her test hasn't come back yet. Thanks for teaching us about protecting ourselves from diseases. Sorry about not telling you about my life sooner. I like talking to you and didn't want you to think awful things of me. Sorry 'bout not telling you to your face. I find it imbarrissing that it was a possibility that I could have had an STD. my aunt said not to be imbarrissd because I didn't get it from sex. I got it from cairing for Grampa. Found out I don't have one. That's good.

Mom walked out on me, left me with Dad. Dad has a girlfriend and sent me to Grandma and Grampa's to live. I wander if anybody does love me.

Trista left school each day for the next two weeks holding hands with a green-haired girl. I'd never seen this before. I had no inclination of her preference. It was a bit sudden.

⊷⊶

Ten days later a round-faced woman with deep-set eyes, a thick head of gray hair, and a slight hump in her upper back leaned on a four-legged cane at my lab door.

Her throaty voice let out trembly words and tears filled her eyes as she told me of her husband's impending death, her battle with cancer, and her son's misguided life.

Students filtered into the lab, but Trista was not one of them. This heartbroken woman forced herself up, using her cane and my arm for leverage, telling me her friend was in the car.

"But we never discussed Trista," I said.

"We don't need to. I know you know. She has a steady girlfriend. And when I die, what will happen to her? Who will support her? We're not trash, you know. It's...well...it's just that Trista needs so much help. We have to walk her through all her homework. And all the reading we have to read to her. We wanted to protect her from the evil of this world. Now it'll soon be over," she said, wiping the corners of her eyes. "I'm dying too." A tear rolled down her cheek. As she toddled out the door, she said, "I just don't know who else loves her besides my husband and I."

"This class loves her," I said. "She has friends here. Most important, Jesus loves her."

"Yes, I know that, but she's not going to school here anymore. She's been moved to a foster home by Child Protective Services. And she doesn't know yet that Jesus loves her. Lord knows I tried."

A week later Trista's grandpa died. And two weeks after that, her grandma died and Trista moved on.

ROUGH EDGES

"What can I help you with, Poppy?" I asked when I saw her long, lean body enter my lab.

She smiled a small, gapped-tooth grin but didn't respond. One of her almond-shaped, dark eyes sat lower on her cheekbone than the other. She dressed in pink sparkly sneakers and a purple jogging suit. Poppy's head was popsicle-stick stiff as she tilted it left.

That was our morning routine.

I kept a sensitive watch on Poppy. Her short-upturned nose. The wide, flat gap between her thin upper lip and nose. Wide-set eyes. Pronounced forehead. The clumsy gait. After three weeks of research in all my nursing books, I recalled where I had witnessed this appearance.

⊶╬⊷

I had been assigned to four-year-old Gideon, a right-below-the-elbow amputee due to trauma at one year of age. His mother had shoved his arm through a wringer washer. She was under the influence of alcohol, as she had been through her entire pregnancy.

He was admitted for a fractured left arm and ecchymosis of his lower legs and face. And there were multiple circular burns the size of my pencil eraser over his chest and extremities.

Gideon was a tiny little fellow with no hair on his head and broad-set, almond-shaped eyes. The groove between his upper lip and nose was smooth. At times his behavior spun out of control. Yet he listened to the directions I gave him. He held his hands over his ears when there were loud noises in the hallway and cowered in bed when the doctor entered the room, but he never whimpered or cried or asked for his mother.

After morning care and treatments, I read to Gideon while he sat on my lap. We rocked, played army with small toy soldiers, and enjoyed building blocks and puppets. Gideon did not know how to play. We worked on that.

I held him tight to me and squeezed him. I visited Gideon in the evenings but never met his mother or father.

I needed more information for my case study.

One of the nurses said, "Oh, you won't see the parents. They have never been here. She's a known alcoholic and drug addict. We have no record of the father."

With time Gideon improved. I wondered who would take him home, hug him, love him. I reported on duty one morning and he was no longer a patient—discharged to his mother.

※+ +※

Day after day Poppy tracked me around the room, tripping over desks and chair legs. She needed individual help with each skill assignment and read a word at a time. She took notes, rewrote the notes, and outlined the chapters, looking for any clue that might allow her to learn. She acted like a student, a student with some odd words and rough edges.

There was a lot of information for her to absorb—maybe too much. Three quarters of it passed right through her undigested. Part of my job was to repeat it until something was learned and attempt different ways of solving problems. I sounded like a preschool teacher.

Poppy's file was thin with only a few bits of information and family history. Five years ago her mother had disclosed that she dealt with alcohol and drug dependence while pregnant with Poppy. She was no longer in Poppy's life. Poppy's father visited her every other weekend when his girlfriend of the week permitted it, but Poppy lived with her paternal grandparents.

"There exists a gap between action, reaction, and understanding the consequences. Physical and cognitive challenges. Requires time with thought processes. Third grade learning level. Refuses further testing and placement," noted Mr. Jacobs, Poppy's middle school special needs counselor.

Mrs. Perry, our special needs counselor, pleaded with Poppy's grandparents to let her level of learning be tested, but they refused. Poppy did not want to be different—labeled.

Two days passed. I asked Poppy into my office for a conference. She recalled the tedious hours discussing her limited mental capacity and remembered the words that silenced her:

"You can't learn. How dumb are you? Face reality, child."

She remembered the Fs that slashed her to the core, the laughter aimed her way on the playground, and not being able to measure height or weight. The words between us were difficult.

Life in my classroom was a constant struggle for her. Poppy arrived with her uniform pants streaked with wet mud from falling while stepping off the bus. Jan, a classmate, had helped her up.

"Everyone has accidents. I keep spare uniforms for this sort of thing," I told Poppy.

In time Poppy began to work more on her own and her skills improved. I rearranged seating and Poppy sat in the front of the class to help her short attention span. Jan helped her read but poor problem-solving skills and inability to assess classmates' sincerity remained, and inability to plan and manage time affected her work production.

Conversation between us progressed. We discussed her uneasiness and social awkwardness, and we looked for reassurances. Poppy shared her anxieties and emotions with me.

"Grandma says Dad avoids me. I guess he thinks of my mom when he sees me. I try all the time to please him. I know he loves me. He's just busy with work. Mom left both of us. Said it was 'cause Dad liked women. I think she wanted alcohol and drugs more than she wanted me."

After five weeks of Jan assisting and encouraging Poppy with her work, Jan approached me after class.

"Poppy writes poetry. I thought you'd like to know."

I stood there and looked at her, trying to understand why she had told me that. And then I recalled a conversation I once had with my English professor. We had talked about poetry, vibrant and tangible—how poetry gives rise to the person or what the person desires.

Poppy shared her journal of poetry with me. She had never shared that personal piece of herself with anyone else, not even her dad or grandparents. I felt honored. It was this journal she later gave me as a gift.

The poems disclosed a vacancy, tenderness, and hurt. Each poem consisted of odd words, awkward verse, and rough edges.

I directed Poppy to write a poem about the skills she was struggling with.

Wash hands
Make bed, unfold shetes,
Put them on soft and sweet…
Sail boat shape I tuck miters,
Oh so tite.
If not teach a frite…

Not knowing what to expect, I had Poppy read it to the class. She stood tall, head up, and grinned. Twenty lines of clumsy.

The class applauded her. I saw a masterpiece. Her grin became a smile. And so, her poems continued. Poppy learned. I updated her other instructors and notated her file.

"Assignments done via poetry give Poppy learning advantage. Although she has a limited mental capacity, Poppy has developed a sense of accomplishment, independence, and value. Passing the home health nurse aide exam awarded her success. Her recent job at a local agency provides her with autonomy and worth."

Poppy will have a lifetime of struggles from alcohol, a lifetime she did not choose.

THE RIGHT DOOR

Tossing my keys into my purse, I walked swiftly to the door with visions of being home. Then I remembered I had not checked email. I scrolled and saw one from a former student, Kate. She emailed me frequently to keep me abreast of her studies and life. This time she had become overwhelmed in her nursing studies and, almost as an afterthought, also requested to interview me for an assignment.

I took a deep breath to revive myself. When life gets hard, it's easy to dislike yourself and develop a negative mindset. Kate was in that pit again, the same one she had been in as my student. Her anxiety threatened to swallow her whole and her mind raced with fear that she was not capable, or worthy, of being a nurse.

As I thought back to class with Kate, I recalled her sleeping, never finishing assignments, and frequently missing school. Something just didn't seem right. One afternoon when I rousted her to get busy in class, her hard exterior had cracked and the sobbing began.

"I can't do this anymore. I'm just going to quit school."

I asked, "How would that work for you?"

Between the tears she answered. "I have job at a Jake's Diner after school for three hours. When I go home I have to take care of my grandma and grandpa. My homework never gets done and I'm failing. I can't even stay awake in class. Why bother?"

"It's your responsibility to care for your grandparents?" I asked.

"Well, I moved here from Arizona to live with them and take care of them. I was living with my mom, but…um…decided to leave."

"What about your dad?"

"He can't do much, either, and he moved out with his girl-friend. He comes over in the day sometimes. But that leaves just me. Grandma can't get out of bed. Grandpa uses a walker. I have to get meals for 'em, change Grandma when she's wet or messy, bathe her…you know, I do it all. Grandpa has to be bathed but at least he can go to the bathroom…well…most of the time. I have to get him up and dressed in the morning before school or he can't get out of bed. He sits in his chair most of day 'cause it's so hard for him to stand, even with the walker. On weekends I have to clean and scrub…oh, and do the wash."

"Kate, there is help out there," I said.

"Really, there's help for them? Dad said I had to do it 'cause nobody helps."

"I take it that your grandparents are on a fixed income? Was your grandfather a veteran?"

"Yes, Medicare and some state funding too. Nope, not a veteran."

"Alright, let me contact a couple home health care agencies and see what they can offer."

It took a few months but help finally came. Kate's grades improved and she became a top student at our school.

I emailed Kate and set a time for the interview. While Kate prepared interview questions, my mind compiled words of encouragement for her. Trying to control her circumstances would never work, but helping her react more positively perhaps would open her eyes.

I scrolled through all the emails I had received from Kate over the past five years. She always started by asking about me, then shared the ups and downs of her home life—Grandma passing, Dad now needing care, and Mom back from Arizona. Her studies were the bright spot in her life. She enjoyed each clinical rotation and told me about each one in detail.

My thoughts flashed back to Kalen's words. "Well, it's what you do each September, which doors you open."

It was good to hear Kate's voice, but her chirpy, joyful tone was gone.

After the interview I said, "I believe you are smarter and stronger than you think. I always did, but knowing that isn't going to help you get through the next few years of school. You have to keep yourself from sinking. So tell me, what is the real problem?"

"My dad wants me to quit and just take care of Gramps. My Grandma died last year," she said after a moment of silence.

"That would be very nice, but who takes care of your grandfather now?"

"My dad. He thinks I should do it 'cause it hurts his back and he's on disability for it."

"I see. So do you feel guilty about being in school?"

"Oh, I'm so torn between Gramps and my dad and school. I take care of him when I get home, but I work after class. Yes, I guess I am guilty about that and failing."

"Kate, you're trapped with obligations and responsibilities that you should or must do. You need a way out. Why don't you try listing all the pros and cons of taking care of your grandfather, of going to school, and of working? That way you'll see it in front of you and be able to make some changes in your life."

"You had us do that all the time in school. I forgot about it. I suppose I could try."

I didn't hear from Kate again for over a year.

"I know I haven't talked with you in a while, so I thought I'd drop you a few lines," she wrote. "Are you going to be home for Thanksgiving? I want to visit and tell you everything about college and how much I now love it. We started a new rotation at the hospital! This past week was my first week in emergency services and I love it."

Kate's life reminded me of a tree, each branch making a distinction as it grows, each an individual choice—her choice.

Kate matured, seeming to have a better grasp on her stressors and realizing her limits. Last year, she moved to Florida for a position in an emergency room and was earning her master's in nursing.

SOMEBODY

Nobody, that was what they called him. A suitable name. He was not old enough to comprehend what his parents did to him or how he was rescued from their grasp and surrendered to the arms of the loving.

That night, at a parent conference, I met Tyler's adoptive parents, Mark and Judy. I was excited to tell them about Tyler's outstanding class-work.

Mark said, "Tyler's biological mother, Melissa, has a severe learning disorder. She needs help to dress, wash, eat, and stay safe. Her speech is poor and she has difficulty with social skills. We're not sure how or why but she married Christopher, an alcoholic and abusive man. She became pregnant and delivered Tyler. She had no idea she was pregnant, so there was no prenatal care."

That was a lot to grasp.

Then Judy spoke. "When Child Protective Services entered their home, it was horrifying and dangerous. The house was filthy. Dried mud and grass soiled the floors and the walls were covered with splotches of black mold. The odor was sickening—excrement and decaying flesh. Dirty dishes were piled high and moldy dishes littered the refrigerator. The only food in the house was popcorn, dog food, and beer. We saw no dog. The only room, other than the kitchen, was a small, crowded one with two chairs and a TV that blared so loud we had to turn it off. Cardboard boxes mushroomed throughout the room. Newspapers were stacked as end tables. Food wrappers and food debris cluttered the floor."

It was an infectious situation.

Mark reached over and held Judy's hand. After a brief pause, she continued.

"We opened cupboard doors. I tried to open a dull, spotted closet door. It showed water damage and the handle was cold dark metal. It was locked. One of the other workers was able to pry the door open. What I saw was a nightmare. There sat five-year-old Tyler in his four-walled landscape. The stench of his urine and body excrement saturated the air. The blanket he pulled over himself was soaked and appeared never to have been washed. I was overwhelmed."

The entire landscape was destructive.

There were no signs Judy's tears would stop. I told her she didn't need to tell me all that, that we could talk about Tyler's classwork.

She looked at me, then resumed. "There was no bed, no mat—just a cold hard floor. He was skinny, bony to be precise. He only weighed twenty-nine pounds. His diaper hadn't been changed for days and his bottom was raw and bleeding. Other raw areas existed on his elbows and back. Scabs polluted his body along with scars, bruises, burns, and scratches. His mouth was dry and cracked. I tried to give him water but he grunted and pushed my hand away. I noticed plugs of secretions in his nose and tried to remove them. That's when he became violent—kicking, punching, and screaming. The officer struggled to hold him. Handfuls of hair laid about Tyler's four-foot square closet."

Tears welled up in my throat. Judy squeezed my hand.

Mark said, "As the investigation proceeded, we learned that Tyler was more malnourished than initially believed. He was fed dog food."

I was numb.

"Judy's team also uncovered bottles of medication used to sedate little Tyler," Mark continued. "And, by the way, his given name was Nobody. We became his foster parents and changed it to Tyler. He is somebody and he knows that now. Over weeks, Judy's team unearthed more information from neighbors and family. Tyler was fed from two dog bowls on the floor—one for food and one for water. And that was if his mother remembered he even existed. Tyler was beaten by his father if he cried and if he didn't cry. He watched his father drink and shoot up with heroin. He watched his mother smoke crack and get beaten."

With an urgent awareness of the importance of preparing a child for life, Judy wanted to adopt Tyler but Mark was hesitant. When the adoption was final, Judy quit work.

She explained. "It's been a struggle for us. Tyler could not utter a single rational syllable. When he wanted something, he yelled and pounded the floor. I just wanted the tiniest peek of love—a hug or even to have him hold my hand—but he built such walls."

"Soiling his underwear continued for several years," Mark said. "He ate with his fingers and threw his body on the floor in temper tantrums. He threw anything in sight at anyone near. I read to him. It was hard. In time Tyler absorbed the roar of our words. He seemed to enjoy the cadence of our laughter. I caught him in a word now and again. It was a progress of kind and an answer to prayers. We did pray a lot. With the help of our church family, Tyler is who he is today, a devoted Christian. He smiles, talks, and laughs."

That was the Tyler I knew, every defeat and imperfection removed.

The wedding ceremony took place in Central Church gardens, overlooking Williwaw Lake. A harp played soft gentle tones of love—Bach, Handel, and Pachelbel. The family was seated and the piano and trumpets rang out the "Bridal Chorus" as a young lady in a white ball gown with a sweep train, ruffles, and bows walked down the aisle in white pumps. She wore a headband of pearls to match her earrings and necklace and carried a bouquet of calla lilies laced with ferns, wrapped with a satin ribbon. Off to the side five young men walked in stride, as military men do—heroic and noble.

After the final prayer and presentation of the newly joined Mr. and Mrs., the wedding party filed out to "Ode to Joy" and guests moved to another section of the garden where tables and chairs were spaced among the delicate flowers and shrubs. Lovely.

Tyler sat in the empty chair beside me. He talked about boot camp, training, friends, and how he met Paris. And he detailed their dreams for the future. We reminisced about his classroom antics and laughed.

It seemed like yesterday when he had approached me to ask something private.

"I read my Bible every day before school," he had said. "I bring it with me and read it at lunch or if I have any extra time in my classes."

I nodded. I had seen his Bible on the desk.

"I get laughed at and teased. I don't really care. I go on mission trips. I've been to Puerto Rico and Costa Rica with my church. I play guitar in a Christian band. We travel the state and play in churches and at concerts."

He was going to see his birth mother, who was in a mental institution. He asked me to pray for him, for strength.

He had said, "It's simple, but it isn't easy."

I watched Tyler beam with love amidst the roar of congratulations and best wishes. I caught him as he beheld his love, a work of art and love—love so simple but not easy.

The wedding cake sat under a trellis of yellow roses and baby's breath on a white antique desk. Bows of soft yellow satin hung from either side, hooked to the white linen cloth that covered the desk. The wedding cake was cut—three-tiered lemon cake with layered ruffles of citrus icing. Then the groom's cake was cut—two-tiered round chocolate cake with cream cheese icing, decorated to represent the Marine Corps. I noticed an open Bible between the cakes. It joined the couple, binding them together, now and in the future.

Tyler came to my table before he and Paris left for their short honeymoon. I thanked him for inviting me and hugged him.

A week later he deployed to Afghanistan.

UNTIL THEN

When Abigail first knocked on my office door, she was wide-eyed and naïve, tender, ambitious, and full of dreams. But she was having doubts about her faith—the misgivings of a teenager—and she refused to share them with her parents. Then one day Abigail invited me to her church to hear one of her father's sermons.

The building before me was beautiful with its lofty bell tower pointing to the heavens, windows and doors trimmed in white, and the façade edged with brown shingles. An aged stone fence surrounded the building and led to the entrance with twenty-one steps.

The heavy oak door's brown varnish was scratched and chipped and tiny shoe marks smudged the kickplate. Dents marked the entire structure. The brass plated doorknob and faceplate had clouded over time and were covered with fingerprints.

I heard "A Shelter in the Time of Storm" being sung inside. I was ten minutes late.

I opened the door and tiptoed to the sanctuary, slipping into the last pew. The stained-glass windows captured streams of morning sunlight and dispersed them over the congregation.

Pastor Jeffries, Abigail's father, began the Mother's Day sermon. He read from Titus 2:1-10 (ESV). "But as for you, teach what accords with sound doctrine...Older women likewise are to be reverent in behavior, not slanderers or slaves to much wine. They are to teach what is good, and so train the young women to love their husbands and children...Likewise, urge young men to be self-controlled."

His words captured those in the congregation. We sang "I Surrender All" and prayed a closing prayer as the bells pealed.

On the way out I introduced myself. Pastor Jeffries smiled, shook my hand, and thanked me for "being a part, a voice in Abigail's life."

Mrs. Jeffries added, "Our dinner conversations have turned into Abigail telling us about your class. You do have some interesting moments."

⊰⊱

It had been seven years since I'd seen Abigail when I received a letter from her.

Dear Mrs. White,

I'm sitting in this busy airport, waiting on my plane to America for a short visit. I often think back to our conversations in your office when I was so young and wanted to save the world. Well, I still want to save the world but maybe a bit differently now. I'm twenty-five and have grown up.

I do so hope you remember me. I graduated from Liberty College with my bachelor's degree in human services. Yet I continued to struggle with my faith. You remember how

I was? Rebellious, spiteful, not understanding my parents or even trying to plus wanting to go to all the wild parties and find a boyfriend. I was just plain miserable and kinda crusty, like sandpaper. If you remember, Dad made me go to Liberty University. I defied him to send me and he did.

Well, anyway, I remember you telling me to meet Jesus in the pages of scripture and listen to what he was telling me. I thought that was such a hoax. But halfway through my freshman year of college, when life for me was over, I started to read my Bible. I mean, really read it. And one day I closed my Bible and realized that Jesus is the only one who can save the world and that my attitude and how I deal with my circumstances is my choice. The light bulb went on and I knew that whatever situations I faced, God would be with me. That was the day He came into my life. Now, walking with Jesus is the only way I get through my days.

You never knew what your words meant to me. At the time I ignored them, but they never left me. Those words exceeded all others, and you seemed to have perfect control of each word. I should have listened at the time. It sure would've made my life easier.

After I graduated from college, I went on a mission trip to Africa. That journey was hot and thick with bugs on the savanna and it seldom rained, but our mission was beside a river. Violent tribes and animals roamed around the country. I thank God my work lasted only eight months. My hands were calloused from helping the natives plant crops and herd the animals. I'm sending you a picture of our camp and some of the local people I met and worked with.

I returned home where I could eat bagels, strawberries, and potato chips, where I could swim and shop at a mall. Then God called me back to the mission field. I wondered why He would do this to me, send me to Africa and then Asia. I rebelled again. I had life planned—an important career, the perfect husband, two children, and influence. But I recalled my parents and you telling me that life doesn't turn out the way we think it should, the way we plan. My expectations led to more frustration. But I followed and found out God's plans do exceed our expectations.

Five months later I sat on the plane to Asia reading Proverbs 31. It was verse twenty that got my attention. "She opens her hand to the poor and reaches out her hands to the needy." You sent this message to us in class using your own words, requiring us to volunteer and do projects to help the needy. No matter how little we had, there was something we could offer. Now I know why.

I put the letter down to reflect. I thought of our work with the homeless: serving meals and giving clothes to shelters, the fun the students had writing a play about handwashing and creating a stage and puppets for their performance, and the Valentine's Dance we planned for handicapped adults at the county day center. They never complained about doing it all outside of class time.

It is difficult to know what volunteering means to students, but there must be a key to helping others that helps the self.

I picked up the letter and read on.

Asia is where I remain for now. The sun seems to shine all the time. And you'll never guess my responsibilities. I oversee setting up first aid stations and teaching people how to care for injuries, wounds, bites, and anything else that comes their way. Do you remember how I refused to do that in class? It was sickening, but I was just downright mean.

I give the clients vaccines, dress wounds, treat burns, and travel to whichever mission needs me to teach the locals the art of first aid. Others help with building homes and churches, teaching homemaking activities, and cooking. I love these people and my work. The people we work with live in such poverty. They're forced to scrounge for food for their families, they're sick and weak, and children beg on the streets for scraps. It seems impossible to overcome.

I get to unwrap and expose wounds that weep, both physical and spiritual. You know, there are always imperfections. It's Jesus who examines their hearts, unfolds the past, and forgives. I only open a door. One native at a time listens and we share our faith. We become sisters and brothers in Christ.

I am excited about visiting with my family, who is now in Texas. Home is where I'm myself and feel safe and have a spaghetti dinner with strawberry cake for dessert. I never expected that my meaningful moments in life would come from serving God in a not-so-safe country.

I am so grateful that I had you as a teacher. You helped me through my anger, mistrust, and doubts. I hope we connect soon.

Until then,
Abigail

There were days as I drove away from school that I left my ideals, beliefs, and hopes to smolder in forgotten ash, wondering if anything I ever said or did would help to heal any wounds.

Yes, Abigail, until we meet again. God be with you.

PART EIGHT

So I saw that there is nothing better than that a man should rejoice in his work, for that is his lot.
Who can bring him to see what will be after him?

Ecclesiastes 3:22 ESV

THERE COMES A TIME

Sometimes technology is made to sound exquisite by the change it passes along, like the key fob I was handed one day—new beginnings with a stress-free, user-friendly piece of equipment, according to Mr. Arthur, Tech Coordinator.

It made me weary with no jingle of keys, only the *dit-dot* of this remote plastic toy. I looked at the buttons with little emblems—a key, a lock, and arrows up, down, right, and left. I stopped short of jumping on board and put forth a stealth effort to keep my jingly keys an extra few weeks.

Then one day Mr. Arthur entered and moved across my lab in powerful precision. I witnessed the approach of a robot with a fob but thought of Kalen with his keys. I cringed and knew it was over. He expected me to hand him my keys.

The first morning my key fob did not work. I hit the left button, the one with the emblem of a lock. My personal distress signal sounded. I clicked the right lower button, the one with an arrow. The door did not open. I have better things to think about than technology, I thought.

Later that afternoon I realized that my key fob opened a solitary door to a small world and all key fobs had the same shape. In contrast, traditional keys each have a different cut yet they are part of a master, a family connection created regardless of the size or shape, diameter or volume, color or structure. The parts related to create something complex and could open a whole world rather than a single door.

Each key held stories of laughter, pain, education, regrets, changes, comfort, and fear. Some keys carried future successes. "It's just what I do with them each September that counts."

I contemplated how I had arrived there and what I had discovered. It was an unremarkable room with friendships, laughter, and joy and backstories of heartbreak at too early an age, the loss of colleagues, and screams heard in silence. No fob clicked that into reality.

⚒

After twenty years of unlocking all kinds of doors with varying types of keys, I wandered through the lab to my office and sat one more time in the shadows of students and colleagues in the rickety chair next to my vintage desk. All the experiences— planned and unplanned, scheduled and impulsive, delightful and despairing—bonded together. Student challenges were a part of my calling.

Alone with my memories I caught glimpses of Septembers and those uncertain beginnings. Waves of students resembled the rush of a corn field on a windy day. They entered as the reckless, the achievers, the thinkers, the enthusiasts, the defenders, and the chewers. All were shells of sensitivity and faces of promise. All passed through my lab to find their own doors to unlock and worlds to explore. They sought suitable careers for their lives and found a weaving together with other lives.

The last days of a school year are written as a final chapter of each young life. Students face departure from family and inevitable endings that time melts away. The books close as life changes on the end day of these years.

Taking one final look around the room, I said goodbye to that unforgettable part of my life. No students, no books, no book bags, and no papers cluttered the room. Posters, supplies, and equipment were all categorized in storage. The room was lean and stark, as though history had washed away moments and years.

I dissolved into silence. My mouth dried and my eyes watered as I glanced back at my empty room and left it behind, locked.

As I idly walked down the hallway, I passed the Professor's room. He had passed away three years ago, too young, but cancer didn't care. Then there was the library, where I had spent hours learning technology skills. It had been torture for the tech department. I passed the childcare, welding, graphic arts, and partner health care labs. I couldn't possibly count the hours I had spent with my colleagues planning in partnerships, revealing the latest reports, and whispering hearsay. We had chatted about administration—the inexperienced and the dinosaurs—and the decisions they made. We had shared, cried, and laughed together and discussed Child Protective Services and how underpaid and overworked they were and how I tended to be a bit harsh with them.

I stopped in the GRADS office where Ms. Mary and I had helped our pregnant students and shared the pain we heard.

At the main office I reflected on my visits to the superintendent, principal, and supervisor—the leaders who had guided me in my career path. They had facilitated my transition from nursing to education, from school to school, and from patients to students. They had helped me improve my instruction because we shared a vision for education and learning. They had cultivated my leadership and empowered me. Some days I had sought permission and others I had begged forgiveness.

The guidance office loomed ahead. The true concern and compassion our counselors held for each student was immeasurable. Mrs. Gonzalez, the lead counselor, had provided a set of skills I did not have. And when college and scholarship applications were to be completed, Mr. Papas, our do-it-right-or-else guidance counselor, had accepted them no other way but perfect. I had heard many student moans tucked in his office as he helped them strengthen those documents.

This calling, teaching, had infected my very being. My keys, Kalen's keys, had unlocked a vault of pearls—doors to unknown worlds that impacted lives.

I strolled by the custodians' room and said goodbye to Kenny, Steve, Emily, and Buzz. We reminisced, laughed, and talked about the future before the hallway surrounded me in a soft hush.

Nineteen paces to the exit...fifteen...nine. I heard Buzz flick on the scrubber. It groaned as he, smiling and singing, glided it across the tile. Five more steps, then I paused. Why did I ever start this? I must have been mad. Is there ever a finish? Maybe there is no end?

My hand reached the panic bar. I paused again at this door of finality to run down the list of reasons I should not leave and the reasons I should. A crushing fear engulfed my body and pillars of fire stuck in my throat. The loud ticking of the hallway clock hammered in my ear. Who will guide them? Who will teach them?

Behind me I heard the jingle of Emily's keys. She was on her way to lock those doors. I pushed the panic bar and the doors opened—doors of circumstance, one dependent on the other. As I walked toward my car, I heard the *ch'trik*. Doors locked.

Silence.

There comes a season, a time.

EPILOGUE

S ome consider vocational schools and career centers to be
alternative and unconventional forms of education, and they
believe the students who attend them are outcasts—mainstream
disposables. But the real problems are intangible—past experiences, long-held ideas, and mental and/or physical conditions that
impede learning—and they often only persist if not dealt with
properly. Treating only the behavior is like putting a Band-Aid
over a gaping chest wound: it won't solve anything.

Each day I wonder how students learn carrying their beatings
and rapes or knowing Dad's an alcoholic and Mom lives in fear.
How do these children focus knowing they must care for younger
siblings or work after school to financially support the household?
How do students even go to school when they are so ill they can
barely stand or voices tell them what to do? How do they concentrate with no vision of hope, joy, or peace or when they feel unloved
and unwanted or like there is no purpose in living?

The simple answer is they don't.

I appreciate that parents find it difficult to face frailties in their own children, but their reactions to these individual differences sometimes surprised me because I believe we are all miracles of creation and unique.

Many days, life in the classroom is traumatizing, like being struck by lightning, for both educators and students. You see, it's being down in the trenches, directly involved in what transpires behind that closed classroom door, where reality is met and where educators give students hope for success or even just a chance at survival. This is why societal solutions offer little reprieve and often intensify the problems.

Most educators' primary focus is the subject matter they are assigned since students' test scores are used to determine teacher efficacy and the teachers have such limited time to meet subject requirements.

I am a supporter of block scheduling because it gave me the time necessary to accurately assess each student's ability and see each student for who they were rather than just how much they could learn. I was fortunate that my students were with me three-to-four hours each day, yet all the words, tears, and touch could not save the frail or make the sensitive invincible. Students' personal issues, though they may be uncovered by an educator, must also be addressed on a family level and individually.

Education in a classroom won't excite or thrill. It writes no scripts for movies. For some it's too quiet, planned and reserved. But those who educate and love the students leave a bold mark on history, the gift of the future and the selflessness of the human spirit.

I wish I could tell you what transpired in each student's life, but some I never heard from again. And while I may never know how or if I impacted some, I am overwhelmed with hope at the number of my students who have earned bachelor's and master's degrees in nursing, respiratory therapy, physical therapy, and health care administration. These former students now manage emergency rooms, nursing homes, operating rooms, hospitals, urgent cares, clinical units, and free-standing clinics. They are clinical and family practitioners. And one practices chiropractic medicine. Several entered branches of the military. Others have pursued careers in technology, veterinary medicine, animal husbandry, missionary work, homemaking, and horse training.

Twenty years into my teaching career, I faced the most difficult of tasks when retiring and saying goodbye to my colleagues: returning Kalen's keys, the keys that unlocked the meaning of teaching and the hearts and minds of students, parents, and sometimes even administrators.

We, as humans, must recognize that we all have a responsibility to give our youth hope, love, trust, and a sense of security by whatever means we can so they can overcome challenges and not only survive but thrive.

www.ingramcontent.com/pod-product-compliance
Lightning Source LLC
Chambersburg PA
CBHW020151090426
42734CB00008B/777